Ford

Capri

British Library cataloguing-in-publication data:
A catalogue record for this book is available from the British Library.

ISBN 978 1 84425 637 2

Library of Congress catalog card number 2010 924 933

Published by Haynes Publishing, Sparkford, Yeovil, Somerset BA22 7JJ, UK

Tel: 01963 442030 Fax: 01963 440001
Int. tel: +44 1963 442030 Int. fax: +44 1963 440001
E-mail: sales@haynes.co.uk
Website: www.haynes.co.uk

Haynes North America Inc.
861 Lawrence Drive, Newbury Park, California 91320, USA

Printed and bound in the USA

Haynes Enthusiast Guide

Ford
Capri

UGO 207M

Martyn Morgan Jones

FORD CAPRI
CONTENTS

INTRODUCTION   7

CAPRI: THE CLASSIC COUPE

CHAPTER 1   8

FROM MUSTANG … TO COLT …
TO CAPRI

CHAPTER 2   26

THE CAR YOU ALWAYS
PROMISED YOURSELF

CHAPTER 3   54

THE ONCE IN A LIFETIME CAR

CHAPTER 4   70

THE CAPRI III

CHAPTER 5   84

THE RS CAPRIS

CHAPTER 6 92

THE CAPRI IN MOTORSPORT

CHAPTER 7 114

CAPRI TUNERS AND
MODIFIERS

CHAPTER 8 124

BUYING, OWNING AND
RESTORING A CAPRI

CHAPTER 9 138

MODIFYING THE CAPRI

CHAPTER 10 150

THE SUCCESSORS

APPENDIX 156

CLUBS, FORUMS, TRADE
AND SPARES

INDEX 158

ACKNOWLEDGEMENTS 160

INTRODUCTION
CAPRI:
THE CLASSIC COUPE

Given the company's current image, it's hard to believe at the beginning of the 'swinging sixties' the general view of Ford was that of a rather staid manufacturer.

This is all the more surprising when one considers that the company has been involved in motorsport since the turn of the 20th century. It was in 1901, at Grosse Pointe, Michigan, that Henry Ford defeated racing rival Alexander Winton. Indeed, it was as a result of this win – which Henry Ford achieved driving Sweepstakes, a racing car of his own design – that he was able to generate enough financial backing to found the Ford marque. As the century unfolded, Ford's motorsport efforts intensified, especially in the 1950s. Yet, the public still didn't perceive the company as one that produced cars that had a sporty feel, or were appealing to a younger market. However, thanks to a new initiative, and renewed vigour, from the early 1960s, this perception was about to alter forever.

To discover how the company's image underwent such a transformation we must travel back to the America of the late 1950s. In 1957, the Automobile Manufacturers' Association placed a ban on factory-sponsored racing, which posed all manner of problems for the country's car builders, Ford in particular. Almost overnight, any racing with manufacturer involvement became a somewhat covert pastime. Thankfully, common sense prevailed, albeit only after an agonisingly difficult and fraught period had elapsed.

When, in 1962, the ban was lifted, Ford seized the initiative and was quick to implement its 'Total Performance' programme. Conceptualised primarily to improve Ford's production models and revitalise the company's image, the 'Total Performance' programme proved to be a winner. Due to the success of its saloon cars in racing and rallying (the rallying was predominantly a European commitment), Ford soon became recognised as a sporting marque on both the national and international stage, but it wanted an even bigger slice of the motorsports cake.

Henry Ford II had long wanted to see Ford involvement, and success, at Le Mans. Thus was born the GT40 project (which was created as a result of the stillborn Ferrari takeover by Ford). A GT40 led the 1964 Le Mans for a while, won the 1965 Daytona 2,000km, and GT40s dominated the 1966 Le Mans, finishing in a classic 1-2-3 formation.

Ford was taking the fight to the racetracks, and succeeding. And, as a result, it was winning in the showrooms too. Its image had done a rather swift about-turn. Although the GT40 was a major factor changing public opinion, it was the arrival of the Mustang in 1964 that really put Ford on the sporting map and gave the company the image it so coveted.

With its racing successes, and the new Mustang, Ford was now seen as a purveyor of cars that remained true to the company's egalitarian ideals but at the same time oozed speed, power, and raw sex appeal.

And it was thanks to this new image and a fresh outlook that Ford was encouraged, and able, to put new practices into motion that would help lead to the launch of the sporting and stylish Capri. Think Capri, think 1964 Mustang … the two are umbilically linked.

← The Ford Capri
2-litre GT (top)
and 3-litre GT (bottom)
from 1969.
(Ford Motor Company)

← 1968 pre-production
Capri-Colt prototype
(Ford Motor Company)

CHAPTER I
FROM MUSTANG ...
TO COLT ... TO CAPRI

Success sells. The Mustang, which created a completely new market sector, was so favourably received and so overwhelmingly successful that it had only been on sale for a few months before Ford's management mooted doing something similar in Europe. Henry Ford II threw his weight behind the idea, and there were plenty of other Ford people who helped facilitate the Colt/Capri development. However, there are two individuals whose truly exceptional talents, and contribution, stand out – Lee Iacocca and Walter Hayes.

Driven men

LEE IACOCCA

Born Lido Iacocca (he changed his name to Lee when he began working for Ford), Iacocca is a tremendously driven man, with a great work ethic. He is also passionate about his country, despite the racial intolerance he experienced during his younger years. Unable to enlist in the army to fight in World War Two, due to the rheumatic fever he suffered as a child, Lee focused on his studies, enrolling at Lehigh University. After graduating from Lehigh he secured a job with Ford, but decided to put this on hold as he had won the prestigious Wallace Memorial Fellowship at Princeton.

A natural leader and supremely talented, especially with regard to product development, following his graduation from Princeton he began working for Ford in 1946. Having started as a student engineer, Iacocca soon realised that he needed to change direction. Incredibly business-minded and spotting an opportunity in the making, quite early in his career he switched from engineering to sales. The move proved to be productive, although it was only in 1956 that Iacocca's career really began to accelerate.

Ford's sales were down, especially in Philadelphia. To kick-start a sales drive, Iacocca introduced a less financially punitive payment scheme, which featured a smaller down payment and an easier payment schedule. This new initiative, called '56 for 56', made it possible to purchase a new 1956 Ford for just 20% down and $56 a month for three years. The initiative was a huge success. From being at the bottom of the sales charts, Philadelphia rose to the top. So did Iacocca – well, almost. He was appointed as Ford vice-president in 1960.

Another project that Iacocca pioneered was the 'Fairlane Committee'. Although an informal group, the Fairlane Committee included some of Ford's top executives and advertising gurus. Iacocca, who was also the man behind Ford's 'Total Performance' programme, was blessed with an incredibly intuitive mind and an uncanny knack for interpreting trends, and he had a hunch that there was a ready market for an affordable high-performance and sporty-looking car. In 1961 he presented his idea to the Fairlane Committee. His idea was not only approved, it was acted upon.

To decide what type of car Ford should produce, the Fairlane Committee analysed research data drawn from a wide variety of sources. This included demographics which illustrated that there would be an increase in the number of young adults, an increase in the number of two-car families, and an increase in the number of women buying cars. The demographics also revealed that, in general, Americans would have more disposable income. In particular, America's huge 'baby boom' generation was coming of age, and Iacocca pointed out that they would certainly have money to spend – enough money to buy a smaller car that was high on style, generous on space, had sporty features, and was priced to sell.

Based on this data, the Fairlane Committee drew up a set of guidelines for what would become the Mustang. Essentially it had to be compact, but it also needed to hold four passengers. There

← It's in the genes! The Mustang, an American icon, spawned a European icon, the Capri. (Magic Car Pics)

↑ **Fabulous Ford
– the 1964 Mustang – an
automotive icon.
(Ford Motor Company)**

would be a 2,500lb weight limit and the total cost, even with added extras, could not exceed $2,500. To cut down the development costs, and achieve an affordable retail price, the Mustang would have to be based heavily on familiar yet simple components. It was. Much of the chassis, suspension, and drivetrain components were mainly derived from the second generation Ford Falcon, Ford's budget youth-orientated model. They may have been simple, familiar, and not at all expensive, but they were good components. As a result, the whole (Mustang) proved to be much greater than the sum of its (Falcon) parts.

Unusually, the guidelines also stipulated that the new car had to be relevant to a number of market sectors. The consumer should feel comfortable driving the car to work, the shops, church, the drag strip, or the country club. Supplemental to this broad-brush appeal was the requirement to develop one basic car that could be ordered with a wide range of options. This, rather cleverly, allowed the customer to buy as much economy, performance, or luxury as he/she could afford. The end result was the 1964 Mustang, an automotive icon.

Interestingly, although the Mustang ended up as a reasonable-sized four-seater, the production Mustang was far removed from the original prototype. The prototype was in fact a mid-engined, alloy-panelled two-seater with pop-up headlights and a racing screen. Don Frey, who supervised its development, is thought to have seen it as an affordable and fun competitor for the Chevrolet Corvette. At the time, however, the car's most likely competitor was another Chevrolet product, the Corvair Monza.

To generate support for, and interest in, the Mustang project, Dan Gurney raced the prototype at various circuits in America. What is even more fascinating about this car is that under its bonnet was not a V8 engine – it wasn't even a V6. The actual power unit was a 109bhp V4! This 1,498cc 'Cologne' engine, as fitted to the Mustang prototype, was in fact the same unit as would be fitted to the Taunus Ford 12M, and a good number of the German Capris. So even before the Capri was mooted, its DNA was already shared with the Mustang.

The press were smitten with the prototype. Ford, on the other hand, felt that in its proposed form the Mustang would have limited appeal. Sensing that the project was about to be axed, Iacocca seized the initiative and suggested that the Mustang be converted to a four-seater. Against huge opposition (mostly from the company's financial and senior executives, who were still smarting from Ford's Edsel disaster), Iacocca managed to get the Mustang developed and into production.

Not that it was originally going to be named Mustang. Apparently, Henry Ford II wanted to call it a 'Thunderbird II' or 'T-Bird II'. Other names were also considered, including Torino, Turin, and T-5. Some early pre-production prototypes were actually called Ford Cougars and bore an image of a stylised big cat in their grilles. In the end, however, the Mustang name was chosen. There have been a number of reasons put forward as to how it got this name. The 'official' explanation suggests that it came from the fastest propeller-driven aeroplane of the Second World War, the legendary P-51 fighter. However, Ford didn't really want an aeroplane as an emblem, so the horse was chosen instead.

Offered in notchback, fastback, and convertible formats, the Mustang's *pièce de résistance* was that it could be ordered with numerous options, which enabled customers to personalise the car to their heart's and their pocket's content. Brochures listed countless trim options. There were autos (naturally), manual gearboxes, handling packages, disc front brakes (!), and a raft of engines, from the 'weedy' 101bhp straight-six which, at a gasp, could just top 90mph, to the potent 130mph-plus 390bhp V-eight. Plus the Mustang soon came to the attention of the tuners. Caroll Shelby took the Mustang concept quite a few stages further and offered the officially sanctioned GT350 fastback, which has become the stuff of legends. The later GT500 would push the performance envelope even further.

The new 'pony' car, the Mustang, was a runaway success and a volume seller. Ford's research had led it to believe that it could expect around 100,000 sales during year one. In fact some 418,000 were sold, and by 1966 sales had exceeded a million, establishing a record that stood for 20 years.

It was the success of the Mustang that inspired Ford to produce a European version of their

Fit for purpose: the Mustang could be a car for all lifestyles. (Magic Car Pics)

↑ **Henry Ford II, a global player. (Ford Motor Company)**

reasons that Henry Ford II grew to dislike Iacocca was because Iacocca was getting much more of the press limelight. The cover of the 17 April 1964 issue of *Time* magazine, which featured an artistic impression of a rather smug-looking Iacocca (he also appeared on the cover of Newsweek the same week), was probably the beginning of the end. It appeared during the week of the Mustang launch. This, and the fact that Iacocca was cited as being the 'Father of the Mustang', apparently angered Henry Ford II. As far as his career at Ford was concerned, it was downhill for Iacocca from this moment on.

Another reason put forward for his dismissal was that Henry Ford II felt that Iacocca didn't appreciate the increasingly global nature of the company and that he wasn't comfortable in Europe. Fortunately Iacocca remained in favour long enough to bring the Colt/Capri into production and to see it safely into its middle years.

WALTER HAYES

Walter Hayes, a former Fleet Street journalist, was another great thinker with a wonderfully intuitive approach to business. He made himself useful to Henry Ford II and the two would forge a happy and productive working relationship. Henry Ford II liked Hayes, and trusted his judgement, hence Hayes' appointment as Ford of Britain's public affairs director.

An exceptionally talented man, Hayes provided Ford of Britain with just the image makeover it needed in the 1960s. He not only elevated Ford's status, but he also succeeded in changing the public's perception of the company. It was still perceived as an automotive giant, of course, but, largely thanks to Hayes, it was developing just the right kind of public image, an image that was more youthful and fostered accessibility. It was this new image that did much to pave the way for the Colt/Capri – as did Ford's burgeoning involvement with motorsport.

From the early 1960s on Ford was on a roll, especially in the UK where it was becoming inextricably linked with motorsport. This was mainly due to the efforts of Walter Hayes. Although he had been appointed to direct and oversee public affairs, he was soon to discover that Ford's motorsports programme was also within his remit.

'personal coupe'. In 1965, 'Project Colt' was initiated with the sole aim of designing a car with a similar feel to the Mustang, but for the European market, and the UK and Germany in particular.

Iacocca may have been somewhat single-minded, but his management style was far from solitary. He used good marketing research data and he used it well. He surrounded himself with good people. More importantly, he was willing to listen to them. He was also willing to take the risk of introducing a new product. All of these factors combined to make the Mustang a success, and Lee Iacocca became known as the Father of the Mustang. Unfortunately, amongst other things this accolade would eventually lead to his departure from Ford.

Henry Ford II appreciated Iacocca's many qualities, but in 1978, following a number of personal disputes and issues, he dispensed with his services. When asked why he took this drastic course of action, Henry Ford II simply replied: 'Sometimes you just don't like somebody.'

Of course, egos and their relative sizes played a major part in Iacocca's dismissal. One of the

Hirons

512682150

Until Hayes' arrival, Ford of Britain had only dipped its toe in the pool of motorsport; but with Hayes at the helm, Ford became fully immersed and hugely successful. Of course, it was Hayes who brought Ford, Lotus, and the Cortina together. The Lotus Cortina, and indeed Ford, owes a huge debt of gratitude to Hayes. This 'hot-shot' saloon did much to raise Ford's image in Britain and change the public's view of

Hayes also brought Ford into the glamorous and high-octane world of Formula 1. It was thanks largely to him that in 1965 Ford provided £100,000 of funding for Keith Duckworth and Cosworth Engineering to develop its DFV Formula 1 engine. Launched in 1967, and winning its first-ever race (in Jim Clark's Lotus 49 at Zandvoort), the DFV turned out to be the most successful Grand Prix engine ever. Sixteen years after its first win, it notched up win number 155.

↑ **Early design sketches. Top sketch clearly shows the soon-to-be trademark 'hockey stick' body line.** (Ford Motor Company)

F. MAYHEN 67

↑ The Mustang's design heritage is clearly evident ... as are the 'fake' louvres. (Ford Motor Company)

The DFV proved to be a PR triumph for Ford. It proved to be equally positive for Hayes who, thanks to such initiatives, would rise through Ford's ranks.

Europe beckons

Having had a great deal of success with the Mustang, a car which exceeded all expectations and even made the usually stony-faced money men smile, an all-European sporting coupe aimed at the burgeoning 'lifestyle' market made perfect sense. Although the car-buying habits and automotive culture in America were vastly different, the Dearborn management was confident that the Mustang formula would work in the UK and Europe. History has recorded that it did, especially during its first phase when the Capri's design, execution, and concept were at their most pure and, arguably, most attractive. The same can also be said of the Mustang.

Interestingly, by the time the Capri arrived in 1969 the Mustang had ballooned in weight and was losing its way ... and its appeal. The Capri certainly owes much to the Mustang, but only

the original and unsullied version. It changed over the years and moved with the times, but the Capri never lost its focus or direction.

Despite being part of the same parent company, Ford of Britain and Ford of Germany had always been quite separate institutions. Both had been busy developing competing model lines. There was little in the way of liaison. Indeed, it was pretty much a case of 'us' and 'them'. This antipathy towards each other, and the inevitable stilted working relationship, made little business sense and did nothing for globalisation and unification. Over a period of time this state of affairs would change but, in its formative years, the Colt was an Anglo/American project and not an Anglo/German one. The Colt project would draw heavily upon the lessons learnt with the Mustang and there would be many parallels.

Not only was it named 'Colt' in homage to the Mustang, but its development and design would follow the same no-nonsense format. Like the Mustang, the Colt would be strongly styled, have up-to-the-minute looks, boast plenty of features, have seating for four luggage capacity, be affordable, and have a range of engines and trim to choose from. Plus it would also have to rely on current mainstream Ford models for its component parts.

What this meant was that the Colt's designers would have to raid as many of the existing Ford parts bins as possible. At the time, most of those parts bins would have been labelled Cortina.

Linking the Colt to the Cortina was sensible – and practical too. Costs could be kept to an absolute minimum; and every part would have been tried and tested. There was no danger of the Colt being some highly strung and frisky offspring. Buyers would be safe in the knowledge that although it looked fresh and funky, thanks to its Cortina-derived mechanicals it would be utterly dependable too. That said, the Colt's mission in life was to put the enjoyment back into motoring, or as Ford of Britain's then Chief Executive succinctly put it, 'to put the fun back into motoring by making a personal car which is exciting to own and rewarding to drive'.

A rather long-winded statement ... but it made the point!

Designed to thrill

To make a car fun to drive was relatively straightforward. To make it exciting to own was a tad more difficult. What Ford was intending to produce was a mainstream car that melded the ordinary and the exotic, particularly with regard to its appearance. The new car had to push the styling to its boundaries, but not step over them.

Nevertheless, back in the 1960s car design was a somewhat parochial affair. Ford was undoubtedly moving towards becoming a truly global company, but at this stage there was seemingly little cross-pollination of aesthetics and design, and not much in the way of idea-sharing.

Ford of America, which at the time was focusing on the globalisation of the company, controlled much more than just the purse strings. It controlled everything within the company. To get the project under way but, at the same time, to look at the bigger picture, Ford put the talented Uwe Bahnsen in charge (Bahnsen would also oversee the design of the Capri II and III, as well as the Sierra and Scorpio 1 amongst others).

⬇ **Quite an aggressive design, yet the rear side windows look familiar and a similar bonnet bulge would appear on the Capri III. (Ford Motor Company)**

↑ **Colt fibre modelling,
circa 1966. (Ford Motor
Company)**

Then it issued the Colt design brief to its three
main studios, which were in Britain, Germany,
and America. Although each of the submitted
designs had its merits, it was one of the American
proposals that eventually won through. It won
through not because of any incestuous bias, or as
a result of any undue pressure from above, but
simply because it was perceived to be the best
design. Thankfully time, and sales, would prove
this to have been a wise decision.

With the basic design agreed upon, Project
Colt was given the amber light in July 1966 and full-
size GRP mock-ups of the American design were
created. Ford trialled these in Europe, at 'clinics'
that were held in London, Cologne, Brussels,
Amsterdam, Milan, Hamburg, and Geneva. This
was not Ford paying lip-service to convention. The
Colt had to succeed. During the clinic sessions, the
public's opinions were not only canvassed but duly
noted and acted upon.

Two designs were trialled, the 'Flowline' and
the 'GBX'. To avoid any preconceptions, and to
elicit unbiased responses, the manufacturer of
the designs was kept a secret. Not only this, but
participants were also requested to judge the

styling of the Flowline and GBX against other
(Ford) designs and similar sporting designs from
other manufacturers. On the whole the mock-ups
were extremely well received, especially the GBX.
There were criticisms, of course, and the styling
was subsequently amended.

The major criticism, and the one most
often highlighted during the clinics, was the
claustrophobia experienced by rear-seat
passengers. Curiously, it seems that few of the
Colt's design team had ever sat in the rear of
the car. This was probably because they were
preoccupied with how the car looked. Not that
this problem was down to the designers being too
blinkered. No, it was down to Ford. From day one,
Ford insisted that although the car had to be sold
as a four-seater, it was also adamant that the rear
seat accommodation and the body design should
not compromise the sporty styling. In this respect,
the Colt was always going to be a case of form
over function.

In order to address the claustrophobia problem,
the designers increased the size of the rear side-
windows by squaring them off. This was a slight
improvement, as it let more light in, but the

revision didn't meet with universal approval. Rear-seat passengers still complained of being hemmed in by a large area of metal. Fortunately for Ford, the production date wasn't imminent and there was still time to make design changes.

The solution to the problem was to incorporate more glass area. To achieve this, Ford's designers penned the classic 'C'-shape. Only the final batch of prototypes had the unique 'C'-shaped rear windows but, compared to the previous designs, it is remarkable how much these contributed to the car's overall aesthetics. Interestingly, the design Ford adopted was similar to that used on the Consul Capri. Ford obviously thought that some of the Consul Capri's design cues were worth repeating.

Even with the window revisions successfully completed, and the final design signed off, it took another year before the project actually

received the green light for production. This was at a meeting chaired by none other than Henry Ford II himself.

Colt matures

The planned launch date for the Colt was the autumn of 1968. To this end, Ford dipped into the company's coffers and scooped out £20 million, which it reasoned would cover the development budget very nicely. It didn't! In fact, the Colt's development costs would reach £22 million.

It was at Ford's new engineering and technical facility at Dunton, Essex, where the new car was developed. Dunton was opened on 12 October 1967 by Prime Minister Harold Wilson. This impressive facility, where possible future engines, transmissions, and commercial vehicles are developed, is still at the forefront of Ford's technical development.

At Dunton a team of engineers, led by John Hitchman, set about the project. Hitchman, whose CV also included the Corsair GT, had in fact been responsible for the development engineering on the ill-fated Consul Capri, so he was well placed to ensure that 'Project Colt' would not suffer the same fate. Actually, it is worth considering what impact the Consul Classic and the Consul Capri had on Ford's fortunes, and how the lessons learnt would shape the Colt's genesis.

The Consul Classic and its more stylish sibling, the Consul Capri, were produced by Ford of Britain between 1961 and 1964. Desperate to freshen up its image and move the company up-market, Ford pinned its hopes on these two models. The Consul Classic, effectively the Anglia's big brother, was to pick up the mantle of flagship mid-size car. Unfortunately, however, the Consul Classic 315 was unnecessarily over-engineered and therefore a very expensive model to produce.

And the Consul Classic 315 and Capri had a nemesis. But this wasn't the product of some rival manufacturer – it came from within Ford's own stable. Incredibly, the car that forced the Classic and the Capri into a premature retirement was the Cortina.

The Cortina was designed from the outset to be extremely cost-effective and it yielded huge profits for Ford. True, the Consul Classic did have a reasonable following, and was more luxurious than the Cortina, but the Cortina could do everything that the upmarket Consul Classic could.

Although the Consul Classic and the Cortina were dichotomous ventures, intended for two different sectors of the market place, the boundaries became muddied. Unwittingly, the Cortina straddled both market sectors and offered large-car roominess and performance at a very attractive price. It was unprecedented value for money, and sold like the proverbial hot cakes, whereas the Consul Classic sold like yesterday's stale bread, with just 111,225 finding buyers in just over three years.

Then we have to consider the Consul Capri, the Classic's younger and fresher-faced sibling. The Consul Capri was the company's first attempt to follow the successful American 'personal car' trend. Ford's marketing maestros made great play of this fact, proudly proclaiming the two-door coupe as the 'first personal car from Ford of Great Britain'. But sadly, the Consul Capri was a sales flop. It wasn't a bad car, far from it, but the transatlantic shape (penned by Colin Neal but tweaked by Roy Brown for production) and high cost meant that it found few supporters. Pillarless, with a sweeping roof and distinctive folded-over fins, it had oodles of style … and there's the rub. It proved to be rather too much of a styling departure for Ford's quite traditional (at the time) customer base and just 18,716 were sold.

Ford wasn't about to make the same mistake again, so everything about the new Colt was costed, discussed, trialled, and tested. Public reaction to the prototypes had been favourable enough to make Ford realise that it could actually charge more for the Colt than an equivalent-size four-door saloon. This was despite the fact that there would be less interior space, less luggage

← The Consul Capri was styled with flair, but proved too Americanised for British tastes.
(Magic Car Pics)

↓ An exceptionally good car, the Cortina was practical, profitable, and perfectly formed.
(Magic Car Pics)

→ Colt prototype scale model being placed in wind tunnel. (Ford Motor Company)

↓ Anxious moments as the scale model undergoes wind-tunnel testing. (Ford Motor Company)

capacity, and just two doors. Ford realised that buyers were more than willing to pay a premium for style and exclusivity!

European union

In the beginning, the team at Dunton kept everything in-house. The first incarnations of the Colt were basically rebodied Cortinas. Due to the reduction in weight, the suspension settings had to be revised, but the underpinnings were otherwise stock Cortina. Even the engines were regular production units. Ford had planned to offer a wide range, beginning with the lowly but laudable 1.3 in-line four through to the top-of-the-range 2.0 V4 as fitted to the Corsair. The lusty Essex 3.0-litre V6 had yet to be considered for the new car, although

it had already made a welcome debut in the company's flagship model, the Zodiac MkIV.

The Colt would retain several familial links with the Cortina, but not its floorpan. Despite its use being mooted, the Cortina floorpan soon made way for a new design, unique to the Colt. And the wheelbase was slightly longer than the Cortina Mk2. Even the track was wider, especially at the rear. There is no doubting that until this stage of the project, the Colt was an entirely Anglo-American affair and any German input was only noticeable by its absence. This situation would pertain until quite late in the project's development.

There were many reasons for this of course. For two decades following World War Two, Ford's European operations had been divided. Its two biggest European divisions – Ford of Britain and Ford of Germany – actually competed with each other. Each had its own product development department, and those departments worked on competing versions of similar vehicles, eg the Ford Cortina in the UK and the Ford Taunus in Germany.

It was a crazy situation. Here was a supposedly multinational company, using vast amounts of its

capital to compete against itself. Ultimately, this was a competition that neither side could win. Henry Ford II had, for a long time, wanted to do something about this unsatisfactory state of affairs. 'People want better products,' he said, 'and the best way to do that is to remember there is only one Ford Motor Company and we don't have the resources to do everything twice over.'

↑ **Clay-modelling the Colt's dashboard. (Ford Motor Company)**

↑ ↑ **Colt in the studio. (Ford Motor Company)**

→ Heavily disguised Capris being loaded for shipment prior to the launch. (Ford Motor Company)

↑ Cold hard facts – getting the low-down on the Colt during testing in Norway. (Ford Motor Company)

He had been thinking about an integrated 'Ford of Europe' for some time. By the mid-1960s his thoughts had become actions, and Ford of Britain and Ford of Germany were drawing ever closer. Indeed, they had already put some of their differences aside and collaborated on what became known as 'Project Redcap', which led to the creation of the all-conquering Transit. This was actually the first Anglo-German collaboration, and although not widely appreciated it predated the links formed as a result of the Escort project by quite some time. The new Transit was fundamental in generating a successful Anglo-German working relationship – a relationship which had many benefits for the Colt project.

Ford was appreciative of the fact that the commercial market was a potentially huge money-spinner and both sides were looking at producing a new, medium-sized commercial vehicle. In fact work had already begun on new but entirely separate designs in England and in Germany. Fortunately, and before either project had reached a critical phase, Ford of Britain and Ford of Germany decided to pool resources – intellectual and financial.

Differences were put aside and the result of their happy and fruitful union was the highly successful and iconic Transit van. Launched in 1965, it quickly became an industry best-seller, and thanks to constant development it has maintained that market position ever since. The Transit proved just how well the two sides could work together. The seeds of change had been sewn.

Change was not just important, it was essential. Historically, Ford had overseen its European operations from America, but Henry Ford II not only knew that Ford would have to sever its umbilical ties with Europe, he actively campaigned for this to happen. Encouraged by the Transit's success, and due to his desire for globalisation, in 1967 Henry Ford II, a passionate Europhile, decided to sanction a European-based subsidiary to be known as Ford of Europe. This subsidiary, he reasoned, would provide 'on the scene' coordination of the company's operations in Britain, Germany, and on the Continent in general.

It did. And it also did much for Henry Ford II's credibility. He always seemed to live in the shadow of his grandfather Henry Ford I, but it was Henry Ford II who saved the company in the sombre post-war period, and it was he who insisted that Ford should rebuild its European business interests after the war. Until 1967, Ford's European business strategy and structure was muddled and fragmented. Ford of Europe was his passion and he had realised that the increasing integration of European trade activity would best be served from Europe. However, although Henry Ford II did the groundwork, and paved the way, the man he put in charge of 'building' Ford of Europe was John Andrews, former head of Ford of Germany. Joining Andrews in Germany was Walter Hayes, who'd been appointed as vice-president.

California-born John Andrews had headed up a study group that investigated how a combined Ford organisation might operate within a common European market. Nonetheless, according to Walter Hayes' autobiography Andrews was unconvinced that unification was a good idea and, in his opinion, the two sides would be better off remaining autonomous. So John Andrews might not seem to be the obvious choice. But Henry Ford II could be extremely persuasive, so Andrews accepted the challenge, put his doubts behind him, and got things moving – very successfully, as it transpired!

Ford had already introduced more efficient manufacturing methods, which saw the phasing out of local assembly plants in Ford's smaller European markets in favour of large manufacturing units that would supply the national sales companies with complete vehicles. The 1960s also witnessed the opening of major new manufacturing plants at Halewood in the UK and Genk in Belgium.

Andrews took what had been a casual relationship and made it a permanent one. From 1967 on, and protected by Ford of Europe's corporate umbrella, Ford of Britain and Ford of Germany would become merged and would work together on all future model programmes. There was to be no duplication of effort – just a common goal. This Anglo-German partnership was a ground-breaking move, anticipating the future expansion of the European Community and the introduction of the Single Market.

There was one slight problem, though – the two development and engineering centres, in Dunton and Merkenich, were over 400 miles apart. But this did not remain a problem for long. It was swiftly overcome thanks to the establishment of a company airline, which speeded up communication greatly. Ford would go on to pioneer other methods of communication such as video conferencing. Incidentally, the Cologne Merkenich technical centre, which mirrored the Dunton facility, was officially opened on 20 June 1968, and named in honour of John Andrews.

With Andrews, Hayes, and Iacocca based in Europe, technical centres in Dunton and Cologne, and a new spirit of partnership, the stage was set

← **Testing times in Tunisia – a German-specification Capri and Escort being checked over.** (Ford Motor Company)

and the Colt project was ready to move towards production. Except that there was one not-so-small glitch … the Colt name.

What's in a name?

A lot, as it happens, especially when one considers that the Colt moniker happened to be licensed to the Mitsubishi Motor Corporation and had been used on one of their cars since 1963! Somehow, Ford's searches had failed to unearth this rather important fact until quite late in the day.

Anyhow, a new name was needed, but what should it be? The choice was extremely important, as it had to embody the style and the spirit of the new car. Luckily for Ford, the company did have one name they could use. That name was Capri. Since the departure of the Consul Capri this stylish, likeable, feel-good name had been lying redundant for the best part of three years. So in November 1967 Ford picked it up, dusted it off, and applied it to the new car. It was goodbye Colt, hello Capri. There has also been a suggestion that Henry Ford II and his second wife Christina had enjoyed the pleasures of the Island of Capri whilst falling in love, and Henry Ford II part-selected the name of the new car in memory of those happy times. Whether this is true or not it certainly adds to the romance of the Capri.

Separated at birth

Romance aside, the Capri was designed as a sporting car, and as such it had to possess good handling characteristics and have a suitably low-slung stance, especially at the rear. To get the Capri to hunker down and almost kiss the tarmac was easy. All that was needed were low, short travel springs. These would provide the Capri with the right aesthetics, and the requisite sharp handling too. The problem was that if so equipped, and if driven enthusiastically, four-up, the Capri's ground-hugging chassis would become rather too intimate with the road surface.

In the end, Ford managed to engineer a compromise that produced an acceptable ride/handling balance. MacPherson struts were used at the front, whilst the rear was controlled by semi-elliptic leaf springs and telescopic dampers. Coil springs had been trialled, but their location proved to be too intrusive in terms of interior room and boot space. Axle movement, under braking, was dealt with by staggering the lower damper mountings – ie the right-hand one was located slightly forward, the left-hand one slightly aft – and keeping the axle in check by a pair of radius arms. There was nothing exotic or original about the Capri's suspension, but it was well thought through, thoroughly tested, and worked admirably. The rack and pinion steering, a Ford first, was an absolute delight.

In terms of the basic mechanicals and the bodyshell, the UK version of the Capri and its German opposite number were all but identical. Nevertheless, despite the much-vaunted Anglo-German tie-up with regard to the power units and transmissions, there were marked differences. On the surface, it might seem odd to develop a 'world' car only to then put it into production with two separate engine ranges. However, using 'indigenous' engines during the Capri's early years actually made a great deal of sense from both a practical and a cost-effective perspective.

Promotional panache

Ford planned to launch the new Capri in the autumn of 1968. This didn't happen. For various reasons, the Capri only entered production in November 1968, with the result that the launch was rescheduled for 5 February 1969. This date in turn was soon in jeopardy, however, as a number of Ford's component suppliers decided to go on strike. Dwindling stocks of components meant that the Capri's production line slowed from some 350 cars per day to around 50. But somehow Ford managed to get enough Capris through Halewood's doors to ensure that by the launch date each dealer was guaranteed at least one car with which to tempt potential customers.

Not that they needed tempting. Ford had already pulled off a number of marketing strokes that were pure genius. The Capri had already been unveiled to a specially invited and extremely appreciative audience at a ceremony in Bonn, the German capital, on 21 January. Feedback and rumour as a result of this preview only added to the hype, which was further boosted by the company's next promotional masterstroke, the launch proper. This took place at the end of January, at the Brussels Auto Show, but only on the final day.

The show Capri had been lavishly 'gift-wrapped' in a large silver box, complete with ribbon. Audiences could only glimpse the cars via five TV screens, which relayed images of it … but only for half a second at a time. Understandably, anticipation was at an all-time high, with the result that attendance on the show's final, Capri-launch, day broke all previous records by quite a margin.

Just over two weeks after the Brussels Auto Show, on 5 February 1969, and following a huge amount of magazine and billboard publicity, the Capri went on sale across Europe and the UK. Ford of Britain had also gone in for some direct marketing. A number of Capris had been parked in numerous public places, most notably outside the commuter railway stations of southern England. Hordes of jaded commuters would have to file past the strategically placed Capris, which proved to be the perfect 'pick-me-up' – literally!

The Capri was a star, and it could do little wrong for many years to come. Like its progenitor, the Mustang, the Capri appealed to a class of driver whose needs and desires had been ignored for far too long. It was just right for those drivers who needed more than two seats, but still hankered after a sports car, especially one with family-car running costs. The Capri's style, performance, value for money, and character were a revelation and Ford made great play of these qualities in its advertising. This really was a 'personal' coupe. Buyers had the kind of choice that they could hitherto only have dreamt of. The Capri provided bespoke tailoring at an off-the-peg price. 'Make your Capri what you want it to be', was one of Ford's famed advertising slogans. However, not everyone believed what they saw and read. Nevertheless, give or take a little artistic licence, this was not some advertising man's hyperbole. To assuage any fears that the Capri would not be delivered complete, and ready to drive, Ford did its best to put prospective buyers' minds at rest: 'We don't want you to get the idea that because there are so many things you can do to this car, it isn't quite finished when it comes to you,' they said. 'The Capri is a very sumptuous motor car. As it stands. Roomy, comfortable, carpeted wall-to-wall. Fully instrumented. Packed with safety features. And with handling the like of which you've never known.'

Sales rocketed. Creative advertising, celebrity endorsements and, above all, pure talent and style meant that the Capri just flew out of the showrooms, selling twice as many as expected, which amounted to an impressive 3% market share. Ford had stolen a march and its opposition would take years to close the gap.

← **F1 World Champion Jackie Stewart shows off his impressive catch … and the equally impressive new Capri.**
(Ford Motor Company)

Ford Capri: the family-size fastback.

The trouble with most cars that look like the Capri, as far as the family man's concerned is that they're completely impractical.

They're either two seaters. Or two plus two's.

Neither of which is much use if you've got a couple of fast-growing, fidgety kids, a wife and maybe a mother-in-law to ferry around.

The Capri is different. Although it's cunningly designed to look like a racy two seater, there's enough room in the back for two adult-size adults to really spread themselves out.

So obviously you'll have no trouble fitting your kids in.

Nor your luggage come to that. Because the boot's a fair old size too.

There are 5 engines to choose from: 1300, 1300GT, 1600, 1600GT and 2000GT.

So how fast or slow you go is entirely up to you.

One thing all Capris have in common though is a very sporty feel – right down to the low, relaxed driving position.

Finally, we'd like to say a word or two about Capri Custom Plans. This is a method we've devised whereby you can actually have your car tailored to meet your own personal requirements.

Not to mention your wife's. And kid's.

Ford Capri: the car you always promised yourself. From £890.

Recommended retail prices including purchase tax and delivery to Ford Dealerships in the U.K. (excluding N. Ireland) 1300 £890, 1300GT £986, 1600 £936, 1600GT £1,042, 200...
Factory fitted seat belts in accordance with statutory regulations at extra cost. Car shown is fitted with optional sports road wheels available at extra cost.

Capri: the car you always promised yourse

CHAPTER 2
THE CAR YOU ALWAYS PROMISED YOURSELF

Not only was the Capri the car you always promised yourself, it was also the car you could personalise yourself.

At its launch, and for quite some time, there were actually 27 variations on the Capri theme available. Ford hadn't just produced a new car: by providing what it called the 'Capri Custom Plan' it had created an automotive pick'n'mix. By choosing from the wide range of options and engine sizes, buyers were able to 'personalise' their cars. This wasn't simply a car purchase; it was a buying experience. The Capri managed a double-whammy in that it was able to tug at the heartstrings and loosen the purse strings at the same time. The idea behind personalising the Capri came from America, and from the Mustang of course.

To the less blinkered and those more fiscally astute, the options were nothing more than a gimmick and an easy way to garner more cash from the buyer. On a purely financial level this was true, but there was a certain cachet about the options. And it has to be remembered just how poorly equipped the average car was at the time. It was only the influx of equipment-laden Japanese imports that forced the Europeans to up their game.

Power

Although the Capri was now firmly an Anglo-German collaboration, as far as the engines were concerned there was no sharing. This situation would pertain for quite some time.

For the British market, there were initially three engine capacities available. The entry-level 1,298cc Kent engine came from the Escort and could be had in standard or GT tune; the 1,599cc Kent was lifted from the Cortina and was also offered in standard or GT tune; and the range-topping 1,996cc V4 engine originated from the Corsair,

albeit slightly modified due to installation differences. You could only get the V4 in a Capri GT.

Gearboxes and back axles were all sourced from the same range of cars. The 1300, 1600, and 1300GT models received gearboxes from the Escort, whilst the 1600GT and 2000GT utilised gearboxes from the Cortina GT and Corsair 2000E.

By the late 1960s Ford was well established as a manufacturer with definite sporting credentials. When the Capri arrived, rumours abounded that there would be a BDA-engined version in the offing. Enthusiasts were salivating at the mere thought of this performance-orientated model. The Cosworth BDA (Belt Driven Type A) that Ford's public relations department had been raving about was, in effect, a productionised version of the Cosworth Formula 2 FVA engine.

Sadly, however, the Capri BDA only ever reached the prototype stage. Eight were made and all were based on the Capri 1600GT. Blessed with power-bulged bonnets, high-revving, 122bhp, 16-valve DOHC, 1,599cc BDA engines, throaty straight-through exhausts, and running on Minilite wheels, they were a visual, aural, and performance delight. These very hot potential RS Capris amused and impressed the lucky journos who got to drive them at a special pre-launch 'jolly' in Cyprus, but they were never signed off for production. The powers that be considered the BDA engine to be rather too complex, temperamental, and harsh for everyday use. Weight was also a factor. The Escort Twin-Cam was typically around 870kg, whereas the Capri 1600GT weighed in at a rather more portly 915kg. It soon became obvious that a detuned Formula 2 engine wasn't right for a mainstream and heavier Capri. A sensible decision but a shame nevertheless! In the end, to satisfy enthusiasts' needs, the potent Essex 3.0-litre V6 would find its way into the Capri, but not until October 1969, well into the production run.

← **Aspirational advertising.**
(Ford Motor Company)

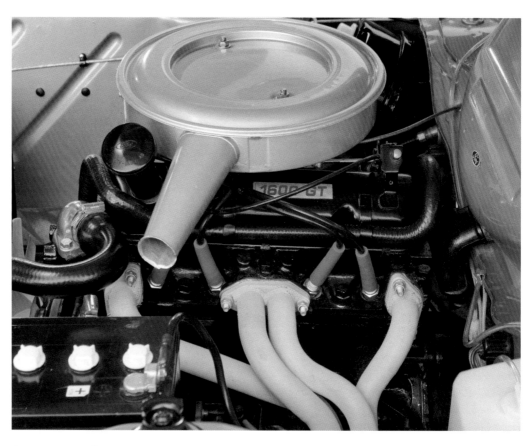

→ Kent 1600GT – the classic choice. (John Colley Photography)

↑ BDA Capris on test in Cyprus (with 'lesser' Capris). (Ford Motor Company)

Style

In addition to the engine choices available, the Capri was very much a style-driven car and buyers could select from a wide range of trim specifications … at a price, despite what some of its creative advertising tried to make you believe.

Ford was a master of the advertising game and it played the game to win. When the Capri was officially launched, the company hit the ground running and placed adverts in the major motoring magazines and newspapers and on numerous billboards. The early marketing strategy certainly made great play of the bargain-basement, entry-level price. Nevertheless, having done so, the narrative soon drew your attention to the various upgrades that were available. Only the impecunious, or Scrooge wannabes, bought the 52bhp base model 1300, which was yours for a measly £890.

True, this was a lot of car for the money. Also true was the fact that it didn't exactly provide much in the way of creature comforts, although it did have efficient through-flow ventilation (as did every Capri). Anyhow, having grabbed your attention with the rock-bottom price, Ford made sure that you were soon tempted by the various options. And, just to show you that it was a responsible company, rather than one that was deliberately trying to coerce you into spending any more than you needed to, it told you so – kind of:

'We don't want to mislead you. £890 buys you the Capri 1300. The 1300 in the picture is fitted with optional sports wheels, which naturally add

← Capri BDA – although it packed a punch, Ford's hierarchy deemed the BDA to be a tad too highly strung for everyday use. (Ford Motor Company)

↓ Stylish, fast, fun, but not for production. (Ford Motor Company)

Ford Capri: £890.

We don't want to mislead you. £890 buys you the Capri 1300.

The 1300 in the picture is fitted with optional sports road wheels, which naturally adds to the cost of the car.

But that doesn't really matter too much. The important thing about the car is this: whichever engine you decide on, 1300, 1300GT, 1600, 1600GT or 2000GT (just for the record, a 2000GT XLR is the most expensive Capri, it costs £1167), your Capri will have 4 things in common with every other Capri.

That beautiful shape.

Enough room in the back for 2 or 3 people to make themselves comfortable.

A good sized boot.

And a very sporty feel to it.

The rest is largely up to you. Because for the Capri we've worked out a system which gives you much more say in what you have in and on your car.

Depending on the version you choose, there's a Capri Custom Plan, that's a pack of extra equipment, which enables you to tailor your car pretty much to your own particular requirements.

Unfortunately, we can't say much about the best part of the bargain. How it feels when you first get behind the wheel of a Capri.

So it... to suggest that you

nip down to your nearest Ford dealer and arrange for a test drive.

All it needs is a quick trip round the houses. You'll come back sold.

Ford Capri: the car you always promised yourself.

CAPRI (Ford)

We were going to call the new Capri a 2+2.
But there's too much room in the back.

We know some people will find it hard to believe that the Capri is a four seater.

It's understandable.

Most cars that look like the Capri are either straightforward two seaters. Or two plus two's. Which in most cases means a two seater with an upholstered shelf in the back. That'll take a bag of golf clubs.

Or somebody small who bends easily. We've gone out of our way to ensure there's enough room inside for 2 adults to make themselves comfortable.

The front seats are deep, wide and sumptuously sprung. The back seats you can sit back and relax in. Without your legs going to sleep. As it stands the Capri is a pretty luxurious motor car.

But if you want to make changes you can. One of the Capri Custom Plans includes reclining front seats and contoured rear seats with a fold-away centre armrest.

Other plans offer other possibilities for personalising your Capri. But one thing you can't do – you can't turn it into a 2-seater.

CAPRI (Ford)

Ford leads the way.

'That beautiful shape.

'Enough room in the back for 2 or 3 people to make themselves comfortable.

'A good sized boot.

'And a very sporty feel to it.'

Very clever! By highlighting these four areas, Ford successfully planted a seed of Capri 'commonality'. Yet the advertisement also drew attention to what you might be missing if you didn't tick some of the option boxes on the order form. Also clever was the way in which Ford's advertising gurus could put a spin on things and turn a negative into a positive. Take the '2+2' advertisement, left, for instance.

Rear seat space was, and always would be, a Capri issue. Nonetheless, by pushing the front seats as far forward as they could go (and tilting the passenger seat backrest), employing an almost anorexic model, and using a wide-angle lens, the rear seat space certainly appears to be on the generous side. However, that's only what the advertisement would have us believe. Any normally proportioned adult who has travelled in the rear of a Capri for any distance knows that it isn't over-endowed with rear headroom or legroom.

to the cost of the car. But that doesn't matter too much. The important thing about the car is this: whichever engine you decide on, 1300, 1300GT, 1600, 1600GT, or 2000GT, your Capri will have 4 things in common with every other Capri.

Most buyers, enthused by the clever advertising, encouraged by skilled sales personnel, and tempted by the delights on display in the showroom, bought Capris with their hearts and not their heads. The Capri was an aspirational car and Ford knew how to tap into this market. They claimed, quite correctly, that at its launch the Capri had more options available than any other British car of the period.

Initially, there were three option packs on offer: L for external accessories, X for internal accessories and R for 'rally' equipment, see panel.

Technically, the X pack (not to be confused with later performance-orientated X packs) could be purchased individually, but in almost every case it was bundled with the L, thus making the desirable XL pack. To encourage XL take-up, dealers typically discounted the price. What you couldn't have was an XR or LR pack.

The R option pack was sometimes referred to as the rally pack. Put the three packs together and you'd get the coveted XLR pack, which retailed at £79 12s 10d. The XLR pack was only available on the Capri GT versions … apparently!

The XLR pack was certainly the most coveted. Due to its price, however, it wasn't the most popular. Few Capris left the factory so well equipped. Most were trimmed to L or XL specification.

The option packs were pretty much set in stone. That's not to say that Ford wasn't averse to massaging specifications, especially if the company

↑ The holy grail of options – the XLR pack. (John Colley Photography)

↓ Sumptuous GT XLR interior. (John Colley Photography)

Ford Capri option packs

THE L PACK
Cost £15 0s 4d. This was the pack for external accessories:
- Identifying badges
- Chrome exhaust trim
- Bumper overriders
- Locking filler cap
- Foot-operated wash/wipe switch
- Bright metal wheel trims
- Bright metal dummy air scoops
- Bright metal side mouldings

THE X PACK
Cost £32 12s 10d. This was the pack for internal accessories:
- Reclining front bucket seats
- Contoured rear seat
- Rear-seat folding armrest
- Extra interior light
- Handbrake-on warning light
- Twin horns
- Dipping and non-glare rear view mirror
- Twin reversing lights

THE R PACK
Cost £39 3s 4d. This was the 'rally' equipment pack:
- Map-reading light
- 5in Rostyle wheels
- 15in leather-trimmed steering wheel
- Matt black bonnet, sills, and tail panel (optional)
- Fog and spot lamps
- Inertia-reel seat belts (£14 0s 9d extra)

← 1969 Capri 1600GT XLR. Pure style! (John Colley Photography)

→ Ford promoted the new Capri when and where it could, the higher the profile the better. This viewing is outside the Houses of Parliament. (Ford Motor Company)

↙ Compare and contrast – you could choose from the 1300L (top) to the 2000GT XLR (bottom). (Ford Motor Company)

↓ Record-breaker! The new Capri even appeared on the cover of this Decca record. The Knokke-Heist song contest, or 'the European Cup for vocal recitation' (as it was actually called) was held from 1959 to 1973 in the Casino of Knokke. Each year, six national teams participated. These are the Belgium contestants.

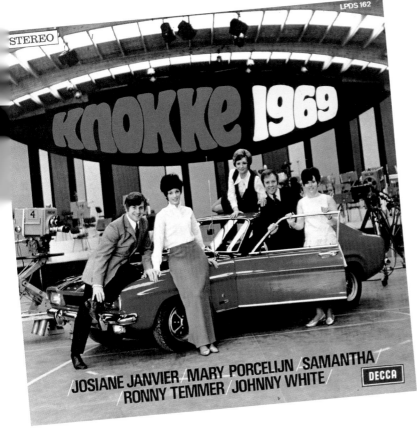

was experiencing a spate of industrial action and/or supply difficulties. The show must go on, and occasionally, when stocks ran low, production-line workers would fit items that happened to be at hand … and happened to fit! Some models would roll off the line with a combination of trim and colours that simply weren't to be found in any of the company's catalogues or sales brochures.

Safety

Despite being an Anglo-European project, the Capri was rooted in America and this undoubtedly shaped it from a visual, performance, and sales perspective. The American links, and forthcoming sales of 'federalised' versions, also helped make the Capri much safer than most of its contemporaries.

During the 1960s, the American public was becoming increasingly concerned over the rising number of traffic fatalities on the nation's roads. Figures had been published which showed that fatalities had increased by nearly 30% between 1960 and 1965. Unless something was done to improve traffic safety, experts forecasted that by

1975 there'd be 100,000 such deaths annually.

Ralph Nader added fuel to the fire when he published *Unsafe at Any Speed* in November 1965. This discourse criticised the automobile industry for neglecting safety in favour of power and styling when designing new vehicles. Its impact was enormous and far-reaching. As a result there was a huge focus on automotive safety in the USA, and the subsequent 1966 National Traffic and Motor Vehicle Safety Act implemented many new rules. These included seat belts for all occupants, impact-absorbing steering columns, padded dashboards, safety glass, and dual-circuit braking systems, etc.

In Britain we weren't quite so zealous about safety, although the situation would improve year by year until by the late 1960s safety features began to sell cars. Saab and, particularly, Volvo had pioneered safety for many years, and little by little other manufacturers followed suit. They not only began to factor safety into their designs, but they started to use them as a marketing tool.

The Capri was a case in point. It featured plenty of crash padding, the steering column had a collapsible section, the wheel was padded, the switches were recessed, the front seats had anti-tipping catches, and the doors were equipped with anti-burst catches, etc. Safety belts were still optional for the European market, though.

In addition a lot of thought had been put into the Capri's structural integrity. The long bonnet was an asset and the front and rear ends were designed to deform progressively in the event of an impact. The fuel tank was not only designed to

↓ **Crash-testing a UK-specification car (top) and a Federal-specification car (bottom) at MIRA. (Ford Motor Company)**

Safety.

There's a lot more to car safety than a bit of padding on the dashboard, seat belts and a good set of brakes.

If a car's going to be safe, it's got to be designed safe and built safe.

And that's what we've done with the Capri. In actual terms there are two kinds of safety.

The first covers all those things that make you less likely to get into trouble.

The second covers what's been done to protect you if you do.

In the drawing we've pinpointed all the major safety features that we've built into the Capri.

Some of them you'll notice as soon as you get behind the wheel.

Like the non-protruding rocker switches, the recessed heater controls and the relocated ignition switch.

Others you'll never actually see because they're part of the structure of the car.

Like the fuel tank. Safely cradled betwee the rear wheels and protected on all sides.

But whether you see them or whether yo don't, one thing's for sure.

In an emergency you've got a lot more th a padded dashboard to fall back on.

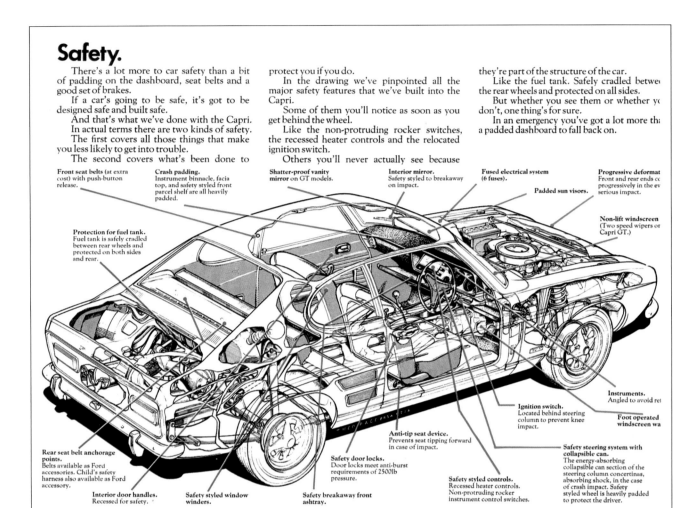

Front seat belts (at extra cost) with push-button release.

Crash padding. Instrument binnacle, facia top, and safety styled front parcel shelf are all heavily padded.

Shatter-proof vanity mirror on GT models.

Interior mirror. Safety styled to breakaway on impact.

Fused electrical system (6 fuses).

Padded sun visors.

Progressive deformat Front and rear ends cc progressively in the ev serious impact.

Non-lift windscreen (Two speed wipers or Capri GT.)

Protection for fuel tank. Fuel tank is safely cradled between rear wheels and protected on both sides and rear.

Instruments. Angled to avoid rei

Ignition switch. Located behind steering column to prevent knee impact.

Foot operated windscreen wa

Rear seat belt anchorage points. Belts available as Ford accessories. Child's safety harness also available as Ford accessory.

Interior door handles. Recessed for safety.

Safety styled window winders.

Safety breakaway front ashtray.

Safety door locks. Door locks meet anti-burst requirements of 2500lb pressure.

Anti-tip seat device. Prevents seat tipping forward in case of impact.

Safety styled controls. Recessed heater controls. Non-protruding rocker instrument control switches.

Safety steering system with collapsible can. The energy-absorbing collapsible can section of the steering column concertinas, absorbing shock, in the case of crash impact. Safety styled wheel is heavily padded to protect the driver.

---

absorb an impact, it was positioned as far out of harm's way as possible. And if it was hit as a result of a rear-end shunt, the tank would ride over the axle and differential.

The Capri fuel tank was so well designed that one was actually fitted to Ford's Experimental Safety Vehicle. It was also considered for Ford of USA's sub-compact Pinto model but sadly never made it on to the production cars. Ford would have a nightmarish time with the Pinto, which despite the new legislation had minimal crash protection and a fuel tank that ruptured if the car was rear-ended (all problems that could have easily been designed out, and the Capri fuel tank would have helped considerably). But the Pinto's quite another story.

There is no doubt that the Capri was everything that the Pinto wasn't. It was stylish and sporty, and, thanks to good product development, extensive testing, and lessons learnt, it was a safe car too.

The V6 Capri

It was not until October 1969 that the range-topping (for the moment) Capri 3000GT arrived, and went on sale with a price tag of £1,291.

There was a good reason for the delay in launching a V6-engined Capri. The 3000GT was a truly sporting car and Ford was appreciative of the fact that it was likely to be driven in a rather more spirited fashion than its larger and lardier V6 Zephyr and V6 Zodiac stablemates. With this in mind, a team of Ford's engineers at Dunton oversaw a programme of Essex enhancement. The trusty V6 became even more trusty thanks to better bearings, a revised oil pick-up, and a baffled sump.

With the engine revisions completed, there was just the simple matter of its installation. Or at least, it should have been a simple matter had it not been for the fact that the twin-choke Weber

↑ Safety sells. Ford was keen to promote the Capri's strong points. (Ford Motor Company)

38 DFAV carburettor, which sat atop the V6, had become rather too intimate with the bonnet. So, as a matter of expediency, the 3.0-litre Capri gained its infamous power bulge. By providing the Weber with room to breathe, Ford had also given the car its very public display of virility. The power bulge would subsequently appear on 'lesser' Capris, but, for a while, this and the trademark twin tailpipes would separate the 3.0-litre from the rest of the mini-Mustang herd. Interestingly, the bonnet bulge actually debuted on the prototype Capri BDAs.

Never the most refined of engines, the Essex V6 was still a very good power unit. It had oodles of character and enough power (albeit not quite as much as Ford claimed it had) to thrust the 3000GT to 60mph in an impressive 9.2 seconds and then let it run all the way to 114mph.

The Essex V6 was actually designed so that

↓ **Ford led the way with the Capri ... and with its clever advertising.** (Ford Motor Company)

We'll sell you your own car.

Our approach to selling cars is rather unique. Let's say you're interested in a Capri.

You walk into your Ford dealer's. The first thing he says is not, "I'm sure you'll like it," but, "How would you like it?"

So you pick up the brochure and tell him. You tell him which engine you want. (There are six you can have. Everything from an economical 1300 to a 3000 GT that'll give an Aston Martin a run for its money.)

You tell him which exterior you want. (A lot of people like our L Pack Custom Plan – metal body mouldings, exhaust trim, wheel trims, locking fuel cap, overriders.)

You tell him which interior. (Perhaps our X Pack – reclining front seats, individual rear seats, additional interior light, handbrake warning light, reversing lights, dual horns, dipping rear view mirror.)

And if you're looking at a GT there's a special Rally Pack you can have on top of all this.

By the time you've finished choosing, do you know what you've bought?

Your own car. We don't expect you to pay for somebody else's.

AMF 367H

← Range-topping 3000GT XLR with period aftermarket Cosmic alloys. (David Morgan Jones)

↓ Plenty of choice! (Ford Motor Company)

it could be used for both petrol and diesel applications. Even though the diesel version never made it into production (in any Ford model), there are elements of 'dieselness' in the design. The pistons are chambered to reduce compression for the petrol engine (they would have been flat-topped in the diesel), the crankshaft bearings are much larger than is the norm, and the construction of the engine is more substantial than it needed to be for a petrol engine – hence its considerable weight.

Having uprated the engine, and power-bulged the bonnet, Dunton's engineers then sorted the chassis. The bodyshell was strengthened, particularly around the side rails, front suspension pick-up points, and top mounts, and the cross-member now had three mounting points instead of two. Stiffer springs, firmer dampers, and harder anti-roll bar bushes were fitted, and wide (185/70/13) Goodyear radials were standard fitment. The battery was also bigger, as was the radiator, and the brakes received better-quality, fade-resistant pads and linings (the linings and drums were also half an inch wider).

To cope with the V6's prodigious thirst for four-star, the petrol tank grew to an impressive 13½ gallons. Mind you, those owners who elected to use all of the V6's lusty power found that even this capacious tank emptied at an all too alarming rate. Another downside was that the larger fuel tank meant a smaller boot. Previously 8.2cu ft, it was now 7.8cu ft.

Silver fox Capri 3000 GT XLR with driving lamp covers, push-button radio but no sports paint scheme.

Sunset red Capri 1600 GT XLR with push-button radio but without sports paint scheme.

Tawny Capri 3000 E.

Sapphire blue Capri 2000 GT XLR with push-button radio, driving lamp covers and vinyl roof.

Evergreen Capri 1300 GT XLR with inertia reel seat belts and push-button radio.

Glacier blue Capri 1600 XL with sliding sunshine roof.

Tawny Capri 1600 GT XLR with fabric trim brushed nylon seats and push-button radio.

Sunset red Capri 1600 GT XLR with push-button radio, sliding sunshine roof and driving lamp covers.

Silver fox Capri 1300 XL with heated rear window.

Sunset red Capri 3000 GT XLR with opening rear quarter vents and quartz-halogen lamps.

Evergreen Capri 1600 L.

Sunset red Capri 1300 GT XLR.

Silver fox Capri 1300 L.

Maize Capri 3000 E with vinyl roof.

Silver fox Capri 3000 GT XLR.

Pacific blue Capri 1600 GT XLR with push-button radio and sliding vinyl roof.

Tawny Capri 1600 GT XLR.

Sunset red Capri 1300 GT XLR.

→ Capri sales were excellent. Many were exported. (Ford Motor Company)

↓ Ford was continually looking at ways to keep the Capri fresh and appealing. This photograph, which was taken in 1972, shows a prototype Capri II at the Piot plant. Note the rear hatch, curious bonnet bulge, and strange grille treatment. (Ford Motor Company)

→ The first Capri special edition – the Capri Special! Ford promoted the Capri Special quite heavily and made great play of the 'spoiler' and 'Lamborghini-like rear window slats'. (Ford Motor Company)

In spite of the compromises and an unhealthy thirst for four-star, the Capri 3000GT had all the makings of a truly great sporting coupe … well, almost all. Unfortunately – especially bearing in mind just how much time had been invested in the engine and chassis – Ford went and spoiled the ship for the proverbial ha'p'orth of tar. How? Well, rather than work the V6 properly, through a close-ratio gearset, and after having gone to

the trouble of making a new gearbox casting, Ford slotted in the ratios from the rather more corpulent Zodiac MkIV. Completing the none-too-rosy picture was a cobbled-up floor linkage and remote change. Not only was this 'bitza' gearbox a recalcitrant affair, it was also saddled with the most unsatisfactory ratios. Unsurprisingly, the Borg Warner Type 35 automatic gearbox proved to be a popular option on V6 Capris.

In March 1970 the 3000GT was joined by the even more upmarket 3000E. The 'E' stood for Executive, which was Ford's absolute top-of-the-range derivative. When you ordered a 3000E, you got the XLR package as well as the delights of a push-button radio, vinyl roof, heated rear screen, opening rear quarter-windows, and cloth inserts for the seats. At £1,513, it was £222 more than the standard 3000GT.

Pricing had actually become something of an issue. Within 18 months, after having listened to criticisms, Ford had dropped a number of the option packs, and many of the previously extra-cost items were now part of the standard specification. And, whereas previously you could order the L, X, and R option packs separately, the only options you could have were the L and XL, although if you bought a GT you could still order the coveted XLR pack.

The range also came in for a number of mechanical improvements at the same time (September 1970). Improved carburation, better cylinder head porting, and new camshaft profiles meant that the 1300 and 1600 engines were much perkier than before. The 1300GT engine now had a very healthy 72bhp. Even the basic 1300 had 57bhp (to be brutally honest, even with 57bhp the Capri didn't accelerate; it just gathered speed). The stock 1600 now delivered 68bhp instead of 64bhp and the 1600GT was blessed with a lusty 86bhp. The other good news was that all Capris, apart from the basic 1300, were now equipped with a brake servo.

With so many Capris to choose from it was no wonder that sales were so good. Buyers were drawn to the Capri like moths to a bright light. In fact, sales were exceptionally good. By the summer of 1970 Cologne had produced 250,000, while Halewood managed 125,000.

Improvements, additions, and changes

For some reason, despite providing a plethora of models and trim specifications Ford felt obliged to offer the rather unimaginatively titled Capri Special (the name was actually chosen by the public in a competition organised by Ford), which arrived in the showrooms during September 1971. Basically a 2000GT XLR, the Capri Special sported Vista Orange paintwork, a vinyl roof, heated rear screen, slatted rear window cover (the Capri is thought to have been the first car to feature this 'must-have' 1970s styling accessory), push-button radio, and cloth trim for the seats. Apart from the lairy paintwork, the car's most noticeable asset was an AVO-inspired matt black rear spoiler, a portent of things to come. Though only 1,200 Capri Specials were produced, it was a welcome but not essential addition to the range.

However, Ford soon realised that it had a more pressing problem than trying to freshen up the Capri's image; it had to freshen up the Essex V6 and try to find its missing horsepower. Despite its 1969 revisions, the Essex V6 engine was still underperforming. Worse still, there had been a number of reliability issues, issues that hadn't arisen (at least not to the same degree) on the typically

less aggressively driven V6 Zephyrs and Zodiacs.

Having initially claimed that the Essex V6 produced 144bhp, this had been amended to 136bhp and then to 128bhp, and even this figure

You can get a Capri Special if you're quick.

The Capri Special isn't the sort of car you come across every day.

We're only making 1,200 of them, for one thing.

And for another, there are few cars around with so much going for them.

For a start, how about 0 to 60 in just over 10 seconds?

A top speed of 106 mph and comfortable cruising at 70 mph.

All by courtesy of the 2-litre engine.

The Special can be dealer fitted with a rear deck 'spoiler' and Lamborghini-like rear window slats.

'Extras' such as push-button radio, heated rear window and black vinyl roof are all standard equipment.

So are fabric seat upholstery and inertia reel seat belts. After all, this is one car that's built for comfort as well as speed.

Finally, with apologies to our founder, you can have any colour you want as long as it's vista orange.

As we said, we're only making 1,200 Specials. So they'll be a bit hard for the average car-buyer to come by.

But then the Special is no average car. Only the real enthusiasts will be after one.

And only the quickest will get one.

CAPRI

...leads the way.

Making a great car even greater...

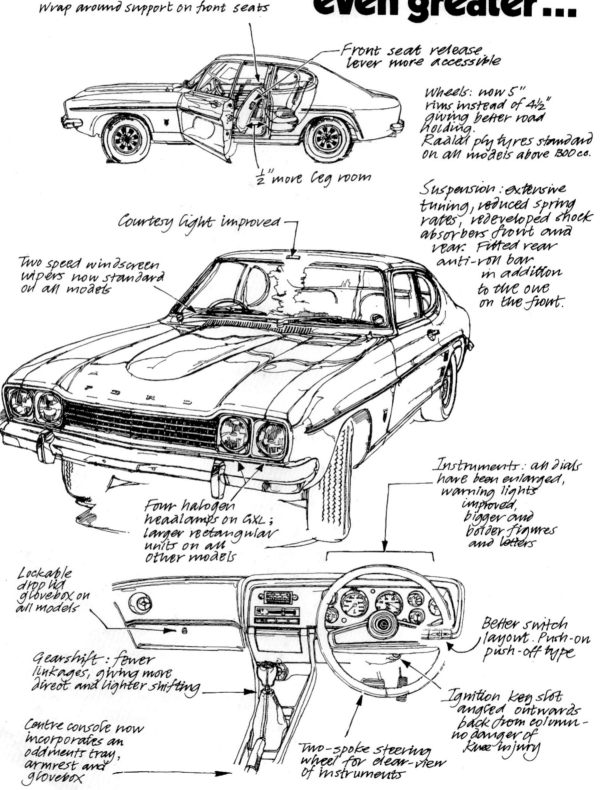

Wrap around support on front seats

Front seat release lever more accessible

½" more leg room

Wheels: now 5" rims instead of 4½" giving better road holding.
Radial ply tyres standard on all models above 1300 c.c.

Suspension: extensive tuning, reduced spring rates, redeveloped shock absorbers front and rear. Fitted rear anti-roll bar in addition to the one on the front.

Courtesy light improved

Two speed windscreen wipers now standard on all models

Four halogen headlamps on GXL; larger rectangular units on all other models

Instruments: all dials have been enlarged, warning lights improved, bigger and bolder figures and letters

Lockable drop lid glovebox on all models

Better switch layout. Push-on push-off type

Gearshift: fewer linkages, giving more direct and lighter shifting

Ignition key slot angled outwards back from column — no danger of knee injury

Centre console now incorporates an oddments tray, armrest and glovebox

Two-spoke steering wheel for clear-view of instruments

was on the optimistic side. A batch of V6s had been bench-tested and Ford's engineers were horrified to discover that some could only muster 121bhp, which was barely 40bhp per litre. Even the 2.0-litre V4 was capable of producing an easy 46bhp per litre.

A new design of camshaft, bigger valves, improved porting and manifolding, re-jetting, a viscous-coupling fan, and a new exhaust system later, the re-energised and more reliable Essex was thumping out a genuine 138bhp DIN. There were other bonuses too. The economy had improved and there were less pollutants being ejected into the atmosphere. And, by softening the rear spring rates, and fitting new front hubs and a bigger servo, the 3.0-litre Capri was quicker around the bends and pulled up more sharply as well. A higher final drive ratio made high-speed cruising even more relaxed, but the icing on the Capri cake was the revised second gear ratio. Ford had finally bestowed the 3.0-litre Capri with the one ratio it so needed, and was moved to boast that the 3.0-litre Capris were the fastest cars that the company had ever sold in the UK. They were!

Ford played the 'keep the Capri fresh card' very well indeed. Having tempted 1,200 buyers to part with their cash for the Capri Special, Ford soon released another batch. Now available in 1600, 2000, and 3000 GT form, the 'new' Capri Special came with inertia-reel belts, opening rear quarters, and a host of other goodies … goodies that would soon find their way on to all production Capris. And the bonnets were now adorned with that thrusting power bulge! With Vista Orange being so last year for the Capri, Ford now offered the Capri Special in two colours, Emerald Green and Ebony Black. Both were partnered with contrasting coachlines in red or gold.

Reintroducing the Capri Special was a very clever move. Not only did Ford manage to cull a lot of its old stock, but it was also able to gauge the market's reaction to the improvements and use this to plan ahead for the next-generation Capri.

In February 1972 the last 3000GT rolled off the production line and in July the last 3000E followed suit. This was in readiness for the new kid on the block, the 3000 GXL, which arrived in September 1972 and took up its position as the premier model in a heavily revised Capri range.

↑ Small changes brought about big improvements. (Ford Motor Company)

The facelifted Capris

Keen to keep the Capri fresh and appealing, Ford introduced the facelifted Capri on 27 September 1972, for all markets. Known almost universally as the Capri Mk1½, it was introduced to the unsuspecting public as the 1973 Capri. As usual, Ford's marketing department had the ability to turn a negative into a positive and it proudly announced that the company had made 151 detail improvements on UK/European cars, 194 on US versions. Quite what the buyers of the Mk1 must have thought, or felt, is probably best left to conjecture.

Easy to recognise due to their bigger, brighter headlamps (quad on 3.0-litre versions) and larger tail lights, the revised Capris were also able to be identified by the new grille colours and designs, which varied depending on the car's status. The dummy side vents had shrunk slightly, and every model except for the base model 1300 ran on radial tyres.

Internally, the Granada-inspired dashboard was completely new, with much clearer instrumentation. The soft-centred, two-spoke steering wheel was also new, and every model had the luxury of cloth inserts in the seats. The

← Funky sketches illustrating the funky design changes. (Ford Motor Company)

front seats even furnished rear-seat passengers with an extra half-inch of legroom thanks to the indented rear panels. Two-speed wipers were now standard across the range. Even the wood veneer was improved. It now looked as if it had actually come from a tree … well, almost. As far as trim options were concerned, in Britain the range had been rationalised. The E and XLR packs were dropped; instead you had to choose from L, XL, and GT, although there was a little more option flexibility than before. Also, it was at this time that the 1300GT and 3000GT models were dropped from the range.

There were mechanical improvements too. On 3.0-litre Capris, the viscous coupling had gained

a friction-reducing Teflon-coated hub, which liberated a bit more power. Instead of 138bhp, the most potent Capris now had 140bhp. Even better news for the 3.0-litre Capris was the adoption of the Consul/Granada gearbox, which had much better ratios and a distinctly less obstructive change. The new 3000GXL didn't disappoint either. Not only was it well equipped (it had most of the R pack items, plus chrome side strips and opening rear quarter-windows), thanks to its American-style quad headlights it also had masses of street presence.

There was a new engine in the British range too, the 1,593cc version of the Pinto (not to be confused with the American Ford mid-size saloon of the same name) that produced 72bhp. In GT tune it had 88bhp on tap. Due to supply difficulties with the 2.0-litre version of the Pinto, the 2.0-litre GT continued to feature the V4 engine, which delivered 92.5bhp.

Regrettably, in an attempt to improve the ride quality all models including the V6 received softer spring rates. The increased suspension travel was welcome, but this made the Capri even more of a 'point and squirt' car than before. Ford had tried to redress the handling balance, but removing the rear radius rods in favour of a cranked anti-roll bar was not a good idea. This device, which was just 10mm in diameter and about half the length of the axle,

was rather ineffectual. It was a case of one step
forward, two steps back.

Sales were still good, however, and the millionth
Capri (an RS2600) rolled off the Saarlouis
production line in August 1973. The last MkI
(MkI½, actually) manufactured at Halewood was
one of a batch of 384 cars that shared factory
space with the Capri II, which was already in
production.

The Capri in Germany

Every engine was a V-configuration 'Cologne',
and there was soon a much greater choice in
terms of capacity. All were drawn from the
fourth generation Taunus range, which had been
introduced in 1966. Initially there were three V4
engines available, which were 1,305cc, 1,498cc,
and 1,698cc respectively. The two potent V6
units, of 1,998cc and 2,293cc, arrived in May. The
V6 engines were simply V4s with an extra two
cylinders added.

Don't confuse the Cologne V6 and the Essex
V6 engines. They may have shared the same

configuration but they are very different animals. The Cologne engines utilise flat-top pistons, vertical valves, and conventionally shaped combustion chambers.

And don't confuse the Cologne engine as being a German design. It was certainly built, developed, improved, and available in a variety of engine capacities in Germany, but the original Cologne engine was actually designed by Ford of America, in Dearborn, Michigan. Its intended purpose in life was as an industrial motor for oil derricks, to power Klieg lights (used in film studios), farm machines, power stations, irrigation pumps, etc. It then went to Europe, where Saab as well as Ford-Koln (Cologne) began to use it. Ford of America had intended to use the V4 in a new medium-sized saloon (codenamed 'Cardinal', after a small red-plumaged North American bird). However, when Ford of America decided not to proceed with the project it was continued by Ford of Germany and would become the new 12M. The 12M was actually the first ever front-wheel-drive car to be built by Ford and its V4 engine was another Ford first.

In addition to having more engine options, the German market also led the way with regard to the high performance versions. The 125bhp 2300GT was launched in September 1969. As well as being the fastest Capri available at the time, the 2300GT held the honour of being the fastest car that Ford had made for the German market.

Trim ranges were all but identical to the UK cars, although the German market seemed to have a predilection for bonnet bulges. In Germany, as in Britain, buyers could choose from the same X, L, and R packs. The R pack (which was adorned with more matt black than its British counterpart was seemingly comfortable with) was only available on the 1700GT and 2300GT models, and, oddly, a special 2.0-litre version, which due to its higher compression ratio was gifted an extra 5bhp.

Probably due to not having to cope with the vagaries of British roads, the spring and damper rates were slightly stiffer, although, as a result, the ride quality on cobbled streets (pavé) was less than good. For some odd reason, slightly smaller diameter front disc brakes were also standard. And, surprisingly, the trademark dummy side vents weren't fitted initially, although they did appear shortly afterwards. However, German Capris did benefit from having a slightly larger petrol tank … which, of course, ate into the already modest luggage space.

Having been able to undertake lengthy high-speed testing on the Autobahns, the Capri

→ **The range-topping and rapid Capri 2600GT. (Ford Motor Company)**

← Early left-hand-drive Capri for the German market. (Ford Motor Company)

rewarded buyers by proving to be a long-legged and remarkably civilised cruiser. Although not whisper-quiet, the Capri had low noise levels. As befitted an Anglo-German project, as well as there being considerable dialogue between the two sides they actually listened to each other! For example, during the high-speed testing the German engineers discovered that the design of the heater allowed rather too much cold air into the cabin. Following discussions, the heater casing was duly modified.

Aside from the trim/powertrain differences that existed between the British and German Capris, there was also the dissimilarity in how the two markets perceived the Capri, and how this affected the way it was marketed. In the UK the Capri was certainly pitched as a sporting car, but there was much more emphasis placed on its pricing, practicality, and everyday usability.

The German market had much more of a technical and engineering bias and the Capri was sold with more of a focus on its sporty nature and its success in motorsport. What was surprising is that the Capri was not fully recognised as a sporting car in the German market and Ford really struggled to get this message across to buyers, despite trying very, very hard.

↑ Capri 2000GT. (Ford Motor Company)

IMPROVEMENTS, ADDITIONS, AND CHANGES

September 1970 was mostly about engine changes and revisions. The 1,498cc engine was up by 5bhp thanks to a raised compression ratio. Sadly, the 2300GT engine, the same unit as was fitted to the Ford Taunus 20M RS Coupe, was out. It had a good track record (a Ford Taunus 20M RS Coupe had won the 1969 Safari Rally), but its time in the Capri was all too short-lived, as it was superseded by the even hotter 2600GT.

↑ New arrival – a golden
opportunity for the Capri
in North America.
(Ford Motor Company)

Although the 2600GT wasn't any more powerful than the 2300GT it replaced, it had a good deal more torque thanks to its stroked engine, which had debuted in the Taunus 26M saloon (its actual capacity was 2,520cc). The 2600GT was introduced in September 1970. At around the same time the 85bhp, 2.0-litre V6 was dropped, although the 108bhp 2300 V6 remained.

During 1971 the trim options were rationalised to be in line with the UK. Possibly influenced by the UK's fondness for limited edition model runs, two such models were launched in Germany. They arrived in the showrooms in 1972. The Monza Blue version was based on the 1500, while the Corn Yellow was a 1700. Both came with sports wheels, plenty of matt black paint, a heated rear window, and a vinyl roof, and 1,000 of each were made.

By far the biggest change occurred in September 1972, which was not only when the facelifted models were introduced but, more importantly, was also when Germany said auf wiedersehen to a number of its vee-configuration engines. The 1305 V4 was replaced by a new in-line 1,293cc, OHC, 55bhp four, which came from the Taunus, and the 1500, 1700, and 2000 engines made way for just one

new engine, the OHC, in-line, four-cylinder, 1,599cc Pinto. This engine was simultaneously launched in Britain and available in standard 72bhp or 88bhp GT tune. Surprisingly, the Essex V6 also found its way to Germany and became top of the range for a while.

The range now consisted of the 1300L, 1600XL, 1600GT, 2300GT (with 108bhp engine), 2600GT, RS2600, and 3000GXL.

By the time Mk1 production had ended, the three plants at Niehl, Saarlouis, and Cologne had churned out around 784,000 Capris. Of these, approximately 240,000 went to the home market; many were exported to America.

The Capri in North America

Considering that 513,449 Capris were sold in North America, which approximated to almost a third of the entire production run, this facet of the car's history is all too often overlooked. And the Americans were only offered the Capri from 1970 (it was first displayed at the New York Auto Show on 3 April) through to the end of 1977. Selling half a million imported Capris in less than eight years was quite remarkable.

Not that the Capri was actually sold through Ford dealerships; it was only available via the Lincoln-Mercury franchise. The rationale behind this decision was driven by common sense. Ford already had the sub-compact Pinto, which, despite its lack of ability and poor safety record, was selling well on the domestic market.

The mistake that Ford made with the Pinto was not purely an engineering one (although the car was designed and developed on an incredibly accelerated schedule); it was also a legal one. Ford had kept documents that clearly indicated the cost-benefit analysis it had undertaken and the subsequent decision not to shield or improve the fuel tank and system. The Pinto had therefore become the focus of much negative attention due to its design, which allowed the fuel tank to rupture in the event of a rear-end collision. To pitch the funky (and safe) new Capri alongside the rather less than attractive and mediocre Pinto would be akin to the company shooting itself in the corporate foot. There is no doubt that the Capri would have stolen sales from the Pinto. Compared to the Capri the Pinto was an automotive also-ran, and it sold only because it was priced competitively and aggressively marketed.

Instead of selling the Capri through its vast dealership, Ford therefore 'gave' the Capri to Lincoln-Mercury. In the USA, consequently, the Capri never carried a Ford badge anywhere on the body. The only place a 'Ford' label appeared was as an inch-long logo on the passenger-side carpet threshold moulding! Lincoln-Mercury dealers also handled the European Pantera sales for Ford (Panteras featured a plethora of switch work, lamps, and assorted minor parts plucked from the Capri parts bins).

Marketing the Capri through Lincoln-Mercury was an exceptionally shrewd move. Until this time, Lincoln-Mercury only really dealt in larger cars. The Capri was a welcome niche addition to the Lincoln-Mercury stable and took centre stage in the showrooms, where it was not in direct competition with any of the company's products. Marketed as an upmarket yet affordable European car, the advertising focused on two key areas. These were the Lincoln-Mercury branding and the Capri's European appeal: 'Capri. The Sexy European. Imported for Lincoln-Mercury.'

The Lincoln-Mercury dealerships were quick to clutch the Capri to their collective bosom, and the stylish newcomer generated a great number of sales and much in the way of showroom traffic. Between its April launch and the end of 1970, 15,000 Capris were sold. This was all the more surprising considering that just one engine was available, the trusty OHV Kent 1600.

There was nothing wrong with this engine – it was willing enough, it was just that when compared to what the buyers had typically been used to, with just 75bhp, it was lacking in the trouser department. As a (relatively) small capacity engine, which was also saddled with emission control equipment, it was never going to set the tarmac on fire. *Car and Driver* was sufficiently moved by the Capri's lack of get-up-and-go to write: 'let the bad part be recorded forthwith: The car is coming to the United States with the wrong engine . . . the so-called federal car is no better than the Beetle in performance, and all this from a $2295 car which

↓ **A sexy European for the North American market. (Ford Motor Company)**

Capri 2000 and Capri V-6. Sexy Europeans Imported for Lincoln-Mercury

Capri V-6 with optional Decor Group shown in rear

looks like it would suck the doors off any of its competition.'

Other magazines would make similar observations. Nevertheless, the mediocre performance was pretty much the only negative response from the automotive press, which took to the Capri like the proverbial duck to water. The reason for kick-starting the American range of Capris with the 1600 Kent was simple. Getting an engine approved for sale in the US was a long-winded and fraught process (which begs the question why this process hadn't been started sooner). The Kent engine was readily available, and had the added advantage of already being 'federalised'. The Cortina Mk2, examples of which had been sold in the US, had almost exactly the same engine.

When, in 1971, the Capri was offered with a 2.0-litre OHC Pinto engine, which is the engine it should have been offered with in the first place, the press was even more smitten. *Road Test* magazine went as far as naming the Capri its '1971 Import Car of the Year': 'Our choice was unanimous when the time for selection came,' the editors said. 'All imports can be categorised as "good" nowadays, and in some years it's difficult to pick a single one that's outstanding. That was not the case this time. We feel that when quality, quality control, appearance, luxury of trim, utility, handling and performance are all evaluated as a "package" at a given price, the Capri clearly shows as the winner.'

↓ **The winning choice. (Ford Motor Company)**

Quite an accolade! Even *Road and Track* had a very public change of heart: 'It certainly is no stone, as astonished owners of Fiat 124 coupes, Porsche 914s, BMW 2002s and fuel-injected Alfas will begrudgingly attest. The Capri will not only out-sprint these traditional heavies on the enthusiast scene, in the hands of a capable driver it will leave them embarrassed in the corners.

'Furthermore, the Capri packs essentially as much usable space and comfort into its compact dimensions as the Mustang after which it was styled. All of these very real assets are yours, wrapped in the color of your choice, for a very friendly price of just over $2600.'

IMPROVEMENTS, ADDITIONS, AND CHANGES

So, the press was impressed, as too was the motoring public. Sales accelerated. By the end of 1971, 53,000 Capris had been sold in the USA. Popular options were an AM radio, vinyl roof, sunroof, and air conditioning. Buyers seeking a little more luxury from their motoring could order the optional Capri Décor Group, which included a sports console with clock, reclining front seats, separate contoured rear seats with a folding armrest, a leather-trimmed sports steering wheel and gear-shift knob, and a map-light, amongst other things. Dual circuit braking and a laminated windscreen were standard on the North American Capris from the outset.

Even if you did spec your Capri with all the goodies, this still didn't disguise the fact that the performance was a little tardy. But it wasn't all doom and gloom. It was during 1971 that buyers were first able to opt for a three-speed automatic BorgWarner 35 transmission (for the 2.0-litre models), and in 1972 the range was boosted by the arrival of the 107bhp Cologne 2.6-litre V6 and the C4 automatic transmission. In fact, in 1972 the Capri enjoyed its longest list of optional power plants in North America: the 1.6L, the 2.0L, and the 2.6L Cologne. Notably, the American market thus received the Cologne V6 well before the UK market. With the V6 engine it was also running the Mustang close. *Motor Trend* said this in its February 1972 issue: 'BMWs, Fiat 124s, Audis, and even Mustangs become fair game on curvy roads. You can rack

The Capri was voted the best Super Coupe offered in America by *CAR and DRIVER* magazine's ninth annual Reader's Choice Poll.

↑ **Stunning 1973 Capri 2600GT as owned and restored by Team Blitz. (Team Blitz)**

back the sunroof, adjust the seat to your normal body conformations, and really enjoy this car.'

The year 1972 also ushered in even more stringent emission regulations, emasculating the 1600 Kent engine, which was now only capable of an asthmatic 64bhp. Little wonder, then, that the 1600 Kent would be quietly dropped from the range at the end of the year.

The following year, 1973, saw Ford sell 113,000 Capris, making it the second-best-selling brand (to VW). The Capri sold more than Toyota, or Datsun, or British-Leyland, or Fiat, or any other brand but VW. This is a considerable achievement. However, 1973 was the high-water mark for Capri sales in America, and it was of course the facelift model. It also debuted unique American-market front bumper reinforcement and filler panels, the door inner impact beams, and revised quarter-vent trims.

Between 1973 and 1974 the Capri gained front-impact and rear-impact bumpers and a rash of other safety-associated modifications, and the 2.0-litre Pinto, its former front-running engine, would soon be dropped. That said, the introduction of the 2.8-litre Cologne ('Arizona') V6 in 1974

redressed the performance balance. This was the first time the 2.8 Cologne engine would be fitted to a Capri. With 108bhp and a good dollop of low-down torque, the 2.8-litre Capri V6 nailed its colours firmly to the performance car mast.

The 2.8-litre Capri was an expensive car, but very popular with enthusiasts and the motoring press. In the opinion of *Road and Track*: 'The German Ford Capri V-6 continues to be one of the bright spots in motoring, even if its price has climbed an alarming $1000 since we last tested it in May 1972. Despite the agonizingly high price, the V-6 Capri remains a very attractive sporting car. It's as solid as a Mercedes, still compact and light in context of 1974 barrier-busters, fast, reasonably economical of fuel, precise-handling and quick-stopping; its engine and drivetrain are both sporty and refined. It's certainly no wonder that Lincoln-Mercury dealers sold nearly 120,000 of them in 1973 – any concerns of the Mustang's displacing the Capri is long since laid to rest.'

Praise indeed, although little did *Road and Track* know that the magazine's writers, along with other American journalists, would soon be writing the Capri's epitaph.

'THE' AMERICAN RS2600

Only one RS2600 was ever officially imported by the Ford Motor Company. It was also the only two-tone Capri ever to be imported by Ford, and was personally ordered by Henry Ford II for his son Edsel. Henry Ford II insisted that the engine was to be EPA (Environmental Protection Agency) compliant, so it came in carburetted rather than fuel-injected form (fuel injection was relatively new and the early systems were engineered with a performance and not an environmental/economical bias). However, it came with RS2600 manifolds and exhausts system, a long throw crank, big valves, and RS camshaft, which pushed the power to around 150bhp. Apparently the engine was modified

post-importation, and almost certainly without Henry Ford II's knowledge.

Edsel drove the car during his last years at college out east, including driving it to such venues as the famous Lime Rock Park racing circuit. The centre console still carries a metal rally plate from Lime Rock that Edsel installed himself. Apparently he once drove the RS to Lime Rock with Ken Tyrrell, of Formula One fame, as passenger.

The body of the RS2600 was reshaped slightly in order to echo the lines of the Cologne racing Capris. The distinctive all-metal flares were the handiwork of Mr Heinz Prechter and ASC (the American Sunroof Corporation), who first worked with Ford on the 1967 XR7 sunroof conversions. Prechter, a German national, was a friend of the

Ford family and very familiar with the Capri and
the RS Program in Germany. Thus his flares are
a tribute to the 1971–72 works competition cars.
In fact, Edsel was inspired to ask for this RS2600
because of seeing successful works Capris in
competition during the 1971 racing season.

After Edsel's graduation from college and his
assignment to a post with Ford Australia, he traded
in the RS2600 and it ended up at a dealership in
Dearborn. John Prosyniuk saw the Capri on display
in the showroom and bought it instead of a new
car – this was back in 1975 – and he owned it for
the next 25 years. Although it remained essentially
the same, he made some minor changes to the
headlamps, air cleaner, and stereo. Michigan, where
the car was based, is known for its severe winters,

so John ensured that the car was well looked after
and garaged whenever possible. From time to time
he also corresponded with Edsel Ford about it.

In 2000, John sold the RS2600 to Glenn Miller,
senior SVT engineer at Ford. Edsel Ford actually
worked with Glenn on the 2001 project to
reproduce the 1901 Sweepstakes Special, Ford's
first racing vehicle (driven by Henry Ford himself
in 1901), during which time Glenn was able to
reacquaint Edsel with his old RS.

Team Blitz (North America's leading Capri
specialist) became involved with the RS2600 in
2002 and restored it to concours condition as
delivered to Edsel Ford in February 1972. The
job was finished just in time on 12 June 2003, and
displayed as part of the Centennial Celebration at

Ford World Headquarters from Friday morning 13 June through to Monday evening 16 June.

The RS2600 was the only Capri on display at the celebration and created quite a stir inside the 'Glass House', as Ford's world HQ (at the River Rouge plant) is called, where many old hands could recall the car when it was first acquired by Edsel. At the appointed time the RS2600 was parked directly across the main entry of the HQ, and the ensuing stream of stockholders, Ford officials, guests, and media personnel had to file past it going in and out of the Centennial meeting. It was the only car to be granted such a premier location and it garnered many enthusiastic and positive comments.

MISSING OUT

Not being given access to the RS cars or the RS parts programme was a huge source of disappointment for the massed ranks of the US press and US Capri enthusiasts, as Norm Murdock (who runs Team Blitz, North America's leading Capri parts supplier and marque specialist) points out: 'We never got the RS accessories program, or the cars themselves. And this bone sticks in the craw of Ford Euro-car enthusiasts in America to the present day. No Focus RS, no RS500 Sierra, no Cosworth Sierra, no Escort Mexicos, no RS2000s, no Puma Racing, zip, zilch! We keep getting bypassed in this potentially huge market for Ford Europe's top of the line products. Meanwhile, irritatingly, in a stroke of reverse unfairness, Ford America sells its top products to Europeans, like the Mustang and the GT!'

The Capri in Australasia

Sporty cars, especially those with big engines, have always done well in the Antipodes. Unfortunately, however, the Capri – even the 3.0-litre V6 versions – didn't really manage to grab more than a tiny share of the Australian and New Zealand markets.

Built in Sydney by the Ford Motor Company of Australia, and advertised with the catchphrase 'The car that reshapes your life', the Capri went on sale in May 1969 and ceased production in November 1972. What this meant, of course, was that buyers only ever sampled the delights of the Capri MkI. Actually, in the early days only the 1600 Deluxe and 1600GT versions were offered.

At least the GT was dressed to thrill even if it didn't truly have the performance to match, as it only had the standard engine. To separate the GT from the Deluxe, it was blessed with twin bonnet stripes, bonnet pins, and a plethora of detail differences. Not that it hung on to its GT status for long, as in February 1970 the 1600GT became rebadged as the 1600XL. Thankfully, the 3000GT – which was badged as a GT/V6 – also made its appearance in February 1970. According to the sales blurb, the V6 Capri was 'The new shape of power for the 70s'. Sadly, rumours of a V8-engined Capri proved to be unfounded.

Having got off to a promising start, sales of all Capris soon began to slow to a trickle. There was simply too much in the way of home-grown competition for the Capri. And, to rub salt into its Antipodean wound, it was coming under attack from the steady influx of European and Japanese imports.

Just 15,122 Capris were made in Australia. The facelifted MkI, Capri II, and Capri III were never officially sold in Australia, although a good number were imported. Surprisingly (probably due to huge discounts), Ford of Australia did take it upon itself to import 50 of the highly desirable and very low-volume RS3100 models, most of which ended up being used in motorsport.

THE CAPRI IN NEW ZEALAND

Due to foreign exchange limits being in force, the first Capris to find their way to New Zealand were either UK- or German-assembled and were private imports. Because private buyers had to have a foreign exchange account, this usually went hand-in-hand with higher-paid jobs. As a result, the cars that were imported tended to be the higher-specification GT (usually in XLR trim) and the 3000E versions. Ford of New Zealand did in fact begin importing Capris from the UK and from the Australian factory. Viewed as a premium sports car, the Capri took its place alongside the locally manufactured Escorts, Cortinas, and Falcons. How many MkI Capris were sold in New Zealand is unknown, but the car was quite popular.

A change of government brought with it the abolition of the foreign exchange limits and a relaxation of the import duty. This witnessed a huge growth in Capri sales in 1973, which coincided with the introduction of the facelifted model. With Australian production having ceased, all models were imported from the UK.

The Capri in South Africa

As in Australia, South African Capris were home-built and the specifications were very similar. A number were rather home-brewed too.

The South African market had a passion for muscular cars, especially those that were equipped with V8 engines. Spotting an opportunity, Basil Green, a very successful racing driver and boss of Basil Green Motors, Johannesburg, got creative … again. It was he who coined the name Perana (deliberately misspelt), which was applied to his entire range of engine-transplant conversions of popular Ford models. The V6-engined Cortina Perana V6, which was based on the Mk2 and debuted in 1968, was the first to arrive. The beauty of the Perana conversions was that they were well conceived and professionally executed. The Cortina Perana was followed by the Capri Perana V6, Capri Perana V8, Escort Perana, Cortina Mk3 Perana V6, Granada Perana V8, Escort XR3 Perana, and finally the Sapphire Perana.

The Capri Perana V6 is likely to have been the first V6-engined Capri produced. Basil Green actually helped Ford with the design and development of its own Capri V6, which ultimately led to the demise of the Capri Perana V6. Not that Basil Green was unduly concerned, as waiting in the wings was its successor, the Capri Perana

V8, a Capri 3000XL that had been equipped with a Mustang 5.0-litre V8 engine.

The Rallye Sport Capris

There have been many combinations of letters used to give a car a particular designation or to identify it as a particular type, variant, or niche model, but in the world of the blue oval there is one combination that stands out. That combination is RS.

Standing for 'Rallye Sport', the RS series of cars are almost universally recognised as a special breed and the holy grail of Ford ownership. The RS moniker was first applied to the Escort RS1600, the first production car to receive the Cosworth BDA engine. Not long after the RS1600 burst on to the performance car scene, the first of the RS Capris – the RS2600 – emerged to tease and tempt enthusiasts … although its primary purpose in life was to enable Ford of Germany to go racing. The RS2600 did a cracking job and would soon hand over the touring car baton to the even more spectacular RS3100. The Rallye Sport Capris are covered in greater detail in Chapter 5.

↑ **Photographed at Warley, this is possibly a RS2600 prototype. (Ford Motor Company)**

> **DID YOU KNOW?**
> Total Mk1 and Facelift production figure: 1,209,100. Production ended December 1973.

CHAPTER 3
THE ONCE IN A LIFETIME CAR

One surefire way to guarantee a run-out model (or models), and/or a restyle, is falling sales. The Capri had hit the ground running, but by 1973 – despite having hitherto been a sales revelation – it was on the back foot, even with the facelift model on sale. Its share of the market in Britain had dropped from 3% to 2.3% – a significant drop, although not enough of a problem to worry the British dealers unduly. Except the Capri was a European car. Over in Germany, where the Capri had previously taken 3.5% of the total car sales, it was now only registering 1.5%. This was worrying enough for Ford to sanction a restyle and send the designers scurrying to their drawing boards. There were other reasons too. Dealers, owners, and the press had long been critical of the lack of rearward vision and the limited luggage capacity. Ford accepted the criticisms, and the general decline in sales. Thus was born Project Diana.

Project Diana was quite a departure from the original design. Gone were the trademark hockey-stick side mouldings, fake louvres, and a myriad of other details. Wider and longer than its predecessor, the Capri II was a gentler-styled, softer-edged, more grown-up mini-Mustang, which offered a smidge more interior space. Suspension rates were softened across the range to give a more compliant ride, anti-roll bars front and rear were fitted to reduce body movement, and, by increasing the diameter of the front brakes and fitting wider rear drums, the braking performance was improved.

Ford had certainly succeeded in creating a fresh-looking Capri with clean uncluttered lines, bigger headlamps, and a greater glass area (the much-criticised rear three-quarter windows were considerably larger, as was the rear window). The larger glass area made reversing a cinch, and the split rear seats (which also folded flat) were a boon. All versions benefited from a 2.3in wider front track, and power steering was offered on the larger-engined models. The changes certainly helped define the Capri II, but the biggest departure from the original concept was the introduction of a hatchback.

Hatchbacks were not at all common in the early to mid-1970s, so the Capri II was something of a pioneer, certainly in the style-driven world of coupes. In addition to making the new Capri an attractive proposition, by redesigning it as a hatchback Ford had also succeeded in making it a very practical proposition too.

However, to compensate for the rigidity lost due to the large tailgate, Ford's engineers had to beef up the rear of the bodyshell, particularly the roof structure. Unfortunately this extra metalwork added weight (around 45lb/20kg) and Ford was dismayed to discover that as smooth as it looked, the revised body style was actually a tad worse aerodynamically than its predecessor.

Running out of options

Production of the Capri II began in January 1974, and whereas the original had a plethora of options to tease and tempt, the Capri II was only offered in L (effectively base spec), XL, GT, and Ghia trim. Not that the Capri II owners wanted for much. Spoked sports steel wheels (optional) soon became standard on the GT and some of the higher-specification variants. The GT versions also delivered more power, had separate folding rear seats, and benefited from extra instrumentation. Ford had much to celebrate and much to promote … especially the arrival of the Ghia branding.

Ford had owned shares in the Turin-based Ghia Company since 1970 and, from 1973 until very recently, the Ghia moniker represented the company's top-line branding for its mainstream models. Owners of a Capri Ghia were comfortable in the knowledge that their cars were much better

← **A car for all lifestyles. With its absence of fripperies, and smooth lines, the Capri II made a subtle yet attractive style statement. (Ford Motor Company)**

equipped than 'lesser' models. Halogen headlamps were standard, as were special alloy wheels, vinyl roof, tilt and slide sunroof, rear wash/wipe, heated rear screen (also standard on the XL), headrests, side rubbing strips, 'Rialto' cloth trim, and push-button radio.

As well as selecting a particular trim level, buyers could still choose from a range of engines. The parsimonious 1,300cc Kent remained, and during this period of economic crisis it actually sold very well indeed. The 1600 also continued to be a volume seller, but the big news was that the largely unloved 2.0-litre V4 had made way for the lusty, potent, and eminently tuneable 2.0-litre Pinto. This very good engine, which had 98bhp to play with, gave the Capri II a top speed of 108mph and punched it from 0 to 60mph in just 10.5 seconds – impressive figures for a 2.0-litre car in 1974, and not too far adrift from the benchmark 3.0-litre.

Although the 2.0-litre Pinto was an instant hit, the aforementioned 3.0-litre Essex V6 was still the range-topper. Bought by enthusiasts whose pockets were deep enough, or who chose to ignore the effects of the fuel crisis, this charismatic

and capable six-pot had been subject to a number of improvements, although it was still mated to the Granada gearbox (all other Capris were now equipped with close-ratio gearboxes). Ford gearboxes were almost universally regarded as being amongst the very best available, certainly in terms of their ease of operation and precision. Nonetheless, for those looking to soothe their way through our increasingly congested traffic network, automatic transmission was an option. Previously only partnered with the V6, it was now available on all Capris for the first time – with the exception of the lowly 1300. The 1300 also missed out on the servo-assisted brakes, which were now standard on every other model.

The Capri II was the right type of Capri for the period, a period where the emphasis had swung away from outright performance towards accessible performance, good economy, and practicality. A less overtly sporting car than its predecessor, the Capri II was nevertheless the car that Ford, and a good number of its customers, needed.

Launched on 28 February 1974, the Capri II drew many positive responses and a lot of sales.

↓ **Capri II Ghia had all the base model's practicality ... but was blessed with lashings of extras and trimmed with quality materials.**
(Ford Motor Company)

LEIGHAM COURT DRIVE

In its first year, 183,000 found homes throughout Europe. Prices varied from just £1,731 (1300L) to £3,109 (3.0-litre Ghia). When John Bolster tested a 3.0-litre Ghia for Autocar in April 1975, he came away impressed:

'The Ford Capri II, as turned out by Ghia, is a very pleasant car with abundant performance that many people would like to own. Fords are getting a bit pricey these days, and this one runs into quite a lot of money. However, it is an attractive vehicle, lavishly equipped and with a cleverly designed body that is as useful for shopping as for long-distance touring. As it has the Ford service behind it, this coupe is just as practical as the ordinary Ford saloons.'

The all-black Capri II GT S, which arrived in June in the UK and would replace the GT in October 1975, was an exceptionally important addition to the range that came at just the right time. Thankfully the fuel crisis was in the throes of subsiding, the economy was picking up, car production was on the increase, and the Capri S was recognised as a celebration of all that made the original Capri great. The Capri was back where it belonged … in front! On sale for £2,330, it is

thought that 2,003 of the Capri S were produced. (As it was first produced for the German market, a more detailed description is to be found in 'The Capri II in Germany' section on page 59.)

IMPROVEMENTS, ADDITIONS, AND CHANGES

To cater to the ever-changing market, the Capri was regularly reinvented. With signs that sales were beginning to slow, 1975 witnessed a revamp of the whole Capri II range. In November 1975 Ford announced a raft of changes and pushed its VFM (value for money) policy for all it was worth. Claimed to reduce the servicing costs by 40%, the Capri II's standard service intervals were now at 12,000 miles, with the oil and minor service intervals remaining at 6,000.

To cater for the impecunious, a poverty-spec base 1300 model was introduced, which made the 1300L look quite luxurious by comparison. The 1300L now boasted sports wheels, reclining front seats, split rear seats, and a door mirror. It was also goodbye XL and hello GL. And, in an attempt to separate the new from the old, this variant received a trim upgrade including sports wheels,

↑ **Even the base 1300 model looked good. And it was even more practical than its more lavishly equipped stablemates. (Ford Motor Company)**

↑ **Various styling exercises were carried out on the Capri. This photograph, taken at the Piot plant, shows a German-registered Capri II with a dual glass sunroof conversion. (Ford Motor Company)**

centre console, clock, more instrumentation, sculpted GT-type seats, a rear wash/wipe, halogen headlamps and, on all models except the Ghia, a smaller 14in steering wheel.

The S, formerly a special edition, went mainstream, and was offered in a range of colours, which must have really pleased all those who had bought the original model! It replaced the GT versions. Although initially assembled in Britain, due to revisions at Halewood S production soon switched to Germany and the car became an import. In addition to now being available in other colours, the S also gained a GRP front spoiler, push-button radio, inertia-reel seatbelts, three-spoked steering wheel, and those garishly striped seats. Ghia (Ronal) 5½ × 13in alloys were part of the package. Thankfully the 3000S now came with standard-fitment power steering, as did the 3000 Ghia. Even if you were a seven-stone weakling you would now not only be able to drive the fastest and most hairy-chested of Capris … you'd be able to park it too!

Of all the S models, it was the 2.0S that proved to be the most popular. In many ways it was the best Capri all round. *Autocar* did a group test and compared the Capri 2.0S against the BMW 320, Colt Celeste 2000GT, Lancia Beta Coupe 2000, MGB GT, and Vauxhall 2000 GLS Coupe, and found in favour of the Capri: 'The Capri as before makes a great deal of sense. It is enjoyable to drive, as a coupe should be; entertainment is after all part of the purpose of such a car. It is also relatively practical, thanks to the hatchback, and accommodating to drive.'

Well-known and well-respected journalist Graham Robson, who ran two as part of *Autocar*'s test fleet, was one of many to fall for the car's numerous charms: 'This, however, is the end of this particular story. After four years, and two different 2.0-litre Capris, the Robson family has finally outgrown the close-coupled four-seater three-door concept. It was with real regret, and a great deal of affection, that I finally let it go.'

Ford was seemingly on a developmental march. From February 1976 the 1300 versions were equipped with the so-called 'economy' engine. In fact, apart from the switch to a Sonic Idle carburettor (which added a shock wave to the airflow to improve efficiency), the engine was otherwise standard and produced a lacklustre 50bhp. With its plain steel wheels, black bumpers and window surrounds (the black detailing actually looked rather good), the base-model 1300 was also a bit of a plain Jane. On the inside you were treated to a rubber boot mat, non-reclining front seats, a one-piece rear seat … and not much else.

In April 1976 all 3000 Ghia models came with automatic transmission as standard. If you wanted a 3000 Ghia manual you had to tick that option box. If you didn't, you got an auto – only around 10% of 3.0-litre Ghias had manual transmission. Previously available with an auto option, the 3.0S was now a manual-only.

The 1970s would prove to be a strife- and strike-ridden decade, and rising inflation only helped to compound the misery. In 1977 the price of a 3.0S was now £4,125, with the rest of the range starting at £2,662 (for the basic 1300) and rising to £5,088 (for the 3.0 Ghia). Unsurprisingly, the 2.0-litre Capri – particularly in S guise – proved to be something of a hit, and stole some of the 3.0-litre's thunder. In real-world terms it delivered almost as much performance, had sharper handling thanks to carrying less weight over the front axle, and squeezed a lot more from each gallon to boot.

The S versions also had a rear spoiler as an option. The interior remained mostly as before, although the seats now sported brightly coloured panels, which were rather too reminiscent of deck chairs!

The Capri II in Germany

In essence, the Capris produced for the German market were the same as those sold in the UK. For the most part, Ford had succeeded in rationalising the range, and there was a much better working relationship between Halewood and Cologne than before. The one major difference between the British and German markets was in how the Capri II was perceived and hence promoted.

In Germany, as in the UK, the Capri was promoted on: technical merit, practical ability and sporting nature.

The Capri was certainly admired for its technical merit. It was also recognised as being a very practical proposition. But unfortunately – and this was despite the success the company was having with its racing programme – the Capri had always struggled to stamp its sporting identity on the market, and it was losing ground to the very capable Opel Manta and VW Scirocco.

Not that Ford was about to give up. With a

renewed vigour, the marketing department (which continued to promote the Capri II's technical ability and practical nature) set about re-branding the car as 'sporting'. And it was the new Capri S which put the 'sporting' back into the Capri.

A CAR FOR THE DISCERNING: THE VERY SPECIAL CAPRI II S

First displayed in March 1975, at the Geneva Motor Show, the Capri II GT S (code-named Midnight and typically referred to as the Capri S) showed exactly what chief designer Uwe Bahnsen had in mind for the range, especially in Germany. The Capri II S

↑ ↑ **A very desirable Capri – the 3.0S.** (John Colley Photography)

↑ **The new seat trim for the Capri S was cheerful, but far from subtle!** (John Colley Photography)

the seats, although these did have gold-coloured 'Rialto' panels. There was a Special steering wheel centre, which was black but with the word CAPRI picked out in gold. Even the horn on the end of the indicator stalk was black rather than its normal alloy colour. And under the bonnet to the left of the slam panel was an extra chassis plate with the letters 'J/P/SPE'.

Of course, what really set the car apart was its trademark gold coachlining (pin stripes down the top edge of the front wings, along the lip of the bonnet, the lower edge of the tailgate, and along the rear valance just below the lights), gold badging, and gold-finished alloy wheels (gold/black inserted and polished RS four-spoke alloy wheels on 1.6- and 2.0-litre models and gold-inserted Ghia alloys on 3.0-litre models).

Launched in April 1975, The Capri S was initially produced as a 1,000-off special edition but, as in the UK, it would soon become a mainstream model and available in a full range of colours (although the stripes/coachlines would remain). By 1977 the S variants had gained front and rear spoilers, and the suspension came in for some further revisions.

Interestingly Ford produced 250 'JPS' Capris for France, where the model was called the 'Blackbird' and each car had an individual gold plaque attached to the dash. Another 250 were built for Switzerland, ten were built for Holland, and one was a special order for Sweden. A number were also built for Belgium. These were badged 'Francorchamps'.

would become one of the most iconic Capris ever, and the only Capri II special edition to be produced.

The Midnight Black, F1 Lotus, John Player Special-inspired Capri II S was a looker, and most definitely sporting. The bodywork, bumpers, etc, were all black. Ford had gone to the trouble of tinting the windows and epoxy powder-coating the brightwork black. Even the interior was predominantly black (albeit a touch too funereal for some tastes), and was exclusive to this model, but it gave out the right message – a sporting message. The headlining was black, so too were

IMPROVEMENTS, ADDITIONS, AND CHANGES

Although the base-model 1300 had switched to the 1300 Kent engine, it was also fitted with a close-ratio gearbox. This was all the more surprising when one considers that it only had 54bhp at its disposal. Perhaps it needed the closer ratios to help make the most of its modest power output! If you owned a 1600 or a 2.3, then you would have had the Taunus/Cortina gearbox. And, if you wanted a 1,600cc you had to choose between the Kent engine and a low-compression 'economy' 1600 Pinto. If you were so inclined the 2.3-litre Cologne V6 was offered in place of the 2.0-litre Pinto. In fact, like the 1600GT engine, the Pinto would soon be quietly dropped from the German range in May 1976. Its replacement came in the shape of a 2.0-litre Cologne V6. Confusing? Certainly! Quite why this happened isn't clear. Was it a matter of expediency, or patriotism? That said, the good old 2.6 Cologne V6 also bowed out and in its place came the Essex V6, which was mated to the Consul/Granada gearbox.

Trim options pretty much mirrored the UK cars although there were some variations. For example, in Germany you could have a 1600 Ghia. In Britain, the smallest engine option for the Ghia trim level was the 2.0-litre. S models were improved in line with their British counterparts.

Goodbye to Halewood and Saarlouis

The writing had been on the wall for some time. In spite of the improvements Ford had made to the Capri II, sales were on the decline – not so much in Britain, where the Capri II was a good seller and made regular appearances in the top-ten listings, but in Germany, where it never quite garnered the support it should have. Worse still, Ford was about to pull the plug on the Capri in America. With a vastly reduced output in the offing, it made economic sense to centralise Capri production. Plus the new Fiesta was coming on line. To make space for this important new car, Capri production at Saarlouis was stopped in 1975. Between August and October 1976 Capri production at Halewood was wound down and production was steadily transferred to Cologne.

From late 1976 on, all Capri production was undertaken at Cologne. Halewood took up the slack left by the Capri's departure by escalating Escort production. The last Capri II to be produced at Halewood left the factory in October 1976. The last Capri II made at Cologne rolled off the production line in March 1978.

↑ **Nearing the end of the line. This photograph was taken at Halewood in 1975. (Ford Motor Company)**

The Capri II in North America

Despite America's burgeoning love affair with the Capri, enthusiasts were denied the arrival of the Capri II until mid-1975, some 14 months later than its debut in Europe. The main reason as to why the Capri II took so long to cross the water was the advent of unleaded petrol, coupled with the EPA's (Environmental Protection Agency) mandate for catalytic converters.

Ford had been heavily fined by the EPA for falsifying emissions data in the early 1970s, and it could not afford more compliance problems and the inevitable negative publicity. So the Capri II had to be specially engineered for US market leaded fuel. This included the fitment of Thermactor exhaust pumps (which enabled fresh air to unite with the exhaust gases, to form carbon dioxide and water) and matrix catalytic devices in the exhaust system. Europe did not face similar mandates until the 1990s. The Thermactor emission control system was installed at the factory; however, it was not unlawful to remove the system after the owner took delivery of the car!

Perhaps the delay explains why Ford allowed Mercury to introduce its own sub-compact, the Bobcat, in 1975. Except that it wasn't Mercury, it was essentially a badge-engineered Ford Pinto that was blinged-up and fitted with different tail lights, badging, and grille.

Whilst it seems strange that Ford wouldn't sell the Capri alongside the Pinto, yet would allow it to be sold alongside the Bobcat, there were good reasons for this. The Bobcat wasn't perceived to be under threat from the Capri, and, anyway, Ford knew that the Capri's tenure in the US was coming to an end. Ford of America would never let the Capri become anything other than a low-volume specialist import, which was a great shame. In many ways the Capri II (and the forthcoming Capri III) had huge potential. And in many ways, particularly from the mid-1970s onwards, the Capri was probably better suited to the American market than the European one. The Capri could have sold in much larger numbers had Ford of America swallowed its corporate pride and allowed it to continue.

As it transpired, the Capri II would be cut off in its American prime just two years after its belated arrival. Nevertheless, it was very well received, especially the potent 2.8-litre Cologne V6 version.

BETTER LATE THAN NEVER

'Once again, then,' the editors of *Road & Track* wrote in July 1975, 'we can report that the Capri V6 is an attractive, competent and enjoyable car at a reasonable price. It goes, it stops and handles, it's well built and it has that sturdy, precise European character that makes it something special for Americans and Canadians. On top of all this, it's a more practical car because of its new hatchback body. A quality European car at a realistic price – what more could one want?'

The Capri II may have arrived, but the 2.0-litre Pinto had now departed, its place being taken by the 88bhp, 2.3-litre 'Lima' four-cylinder OHC unit, which was now the base engine in the line-up. It was also the last all-new engine ever to be fitted to a production Capri.

Switching to this engine made good sense. Catalytic converters were soon to become mandatory and Ford needed an engine that could tolerate unleaded fuel. And, due to the American market's penchant for goodies and driving aids, it also needed to be able to power steering pumps, automatic transmissions, and air conditioning – hence the arrival of the slightly torquier Lima.

There was another good reason for the introduction of torquier engines – weight. The Capri had become more than a tad lardy. According to the sales brochures, a fully specced 1975 Capri II Ghia weighed in at a rather corpulent 2,996lb/1,360kg (26.75cwt/1.36 tonnes). By comparison, a 1971 Capri 1.6 was an anorexic 2,135lb/969kg (19cwt/0.97 tonnes).

IMPROVEMENTS, ADDITIONS, AND CHANGES

The 2.8-litre Cologne V6 remained, although from 1974 it was much changed and featured numerous design improvements that had their roots in the European Group 2 RS2600 race cars. The 2800 engine block was stronger than the 2600, and its heads were redesigned to eliminate the 2600's siamesed exhaust port (the 2800 always had a three-port exhaust, although this was for emissions reasons rather than for performance enhancement).

For the most part the Capri II was getting rave reviews. In May 1975, premier UK motoring publication *Motor Magazine* managed to get its hands on a Mustang II Ghia V8, which it pitched against a Capri II 3.0-litre Ghia. This head-to-head test

↑ Late model
'Le Cat Black' 2.8.
(Ford Motor Company)

made for very interesting reading … especially the conclusion:

'These two cars represent an almost classic case of "horses for courses" in that, though ostensibly the same car, they are completely different and reflect their home market conditions very strongly. The Mustang is soft, plush, and quiet, but its roadholding and handling are poor, whilst American legislation has reduced what should be a powerful V8 to a shadow of its potential self. The Capri on the other hand, is a taut, lively, fast, efficient, sporting car much more in the mould of the original Mustang and yet doesn't lose out much (if any) in the comfort and refinement stakes. What we find so difficult to understand is how the Americans have managed to lose so much useable space in a package that is very little bigger overall: the space utilisation of the Capri is much better.

'On balance then, we would go for the Capri: in our eyes it is a clear-cut and easy winner in this contest.'

Although this was a British magazine, and an undeniably British verdict, the sentiments it contained were echoed, for the most part, by American journalists … if not quite so openly.

From the 1976 model year on, the 2800 engine sported a Motorcraft 2150 carburettor (complete with electric choke) in place of the previously fitted Holley 5200. The intake manifold was redesigned and the heads were changed slightly too. Solid state 'breakerless' electronic ignition was introduced on both the 2800 and the Lima. The Holley 5200 (which featured an electric choke assist, used in conjunction with a hot-water choke) was retained in 2.3-litre Capri IIs.

Specification-wise, Ford offered three trim levels in 1976. These were: Base, S, and Ghia. To these could be added a 'Décor' pack, which provided the owner with such delights as contoured rear seats, embossed vinyl trim, wood-effect instrument panel, opening quarter-windows, carpet on the lower part of the door cards, and a plethora of other lesser extras. For 1977 the very popular S model (similar visually to the UK/German S) was renamed 'Le Cat Black', which, as its name suggests, was predominantly black … black with gold stripes and gold wheels. Later models would run with steel sports wheels. Others included the rare 'Le Cat White' and the even rarer 'Le Cat Crimson'. On the 'Cat' variants, most of the chrome trim was either blacked out or replaced with gold trim. The seats were black vinyl with gold cloth inserts.

Announcing the Capri
RALLY CAT
Lincoln-Mercury's Newest Snarling Machine

The "Rally Cat" Kit Includes:

- Rear deck spoiler
- Side rocker panel striping with Capri lettering
- Black or white twin stripes that extend boldly over the hood, rear deck, and front and rear bumpers

MERCURY
LINCOLN

↑ **A Capri on the wild side! However, the Rally Cat pack was show, not go. (Ford Motor Company)**

twin stripes that ran the length of the car, massively flared arches (which were pop riveted on), air dam, rear spoiler, R/S body decals, and 7in-wide alloys, the Capri R/S was a brash beast of car. It was only available through 15 specialist Lincoln-Mercury dealers, where it was sold alongside the De Tomaso Pantera supercar.

Not that the R/S pack was a factory creation. It was one of American Sunroof Corporation's (ASC, the same company owned by Heinz Prechter, and supplier to Ford and other OEMs) offerings. It was not sanctioned by Ford in any way. In fact, the reason only a few dozen were made before production ended at ASC was that Ford sent a memo to its dealers advising that the extensive metal removal entailed in the bumper rework had not been crash-tested or certified as a safe modification. It was this that put an end to the R/S.

The R/S was joined by another significant private tuner special, the Chastain S/3, offered by Roger Chastain's firm in southern California. As with the R/S, the Chastain was sold at selected Lincoln-Mercury dealerships that contracted privately with Chastain (and outside of Ford's blessing). Both the R/S and the S/3 were mainly done as body-kit builds with wide tyres and wheels. The beauty was largely skin deep, except for a handful of specially commissioned cars. A few were fitted with the AK Miller turbocharged engine. Team Blitz, in America, owns Chastain S/3 001 which was Roger Chastain's original magazine car, and also the first customer car, sold to a Mr Frankenstein (seriously!) in Los Angeles, and then bought back by Roger for his personal collection in the 1980s. The 'Frankenstein' S/3 Capri II has an AK Miller motor, five-speed manual transmission, louvred Chastain 'Shadow' windows, Koni dampers and strut inserts, thicker anti-roll bars, and a limited slip differential.

In 1977, a number of mechanical changes were made to mainstream North American Capris. The most notable was the switch to the Motorcraft 2700VV (Variable Venturi) carburettor, which was henceforward fitted to all 2.8 Capris sold in California.

The new 2700VV managed to meet California's increasingly stringent emissions regulations, had better drivability, and gave improved fuel economy. Ford needed this carburettor to be in volume usage, as the company had invested considerable

For the Capri owner who really liked to be noticed, Ford offered the rather unusually titled 'Rally Cat' pack. This came with twin racing stripes on the bonnet and hatch, a sizeable rear spoiler, and stripes on the rocker panels (the lower portion of the wings/doors). The Rally Cat pack provided the Capri II with a cosmetic enhancement only.

There was even the so-called R/S pack. Beauty is in the eye of the beholder of course, but the R/S pack made the Capri look less like a sporting coupe and more like a tacky fairground attraction. Marketed from 1975 on, the Capri R/S has to be the most in-your-face Capri ever produced. With

sums getting it developed. Unfortunately, even though the 2700VV met all the relevant criteria it would subsequently prove to be too complex and troublesome. The V6 engine also came in for some further attention. Compression was raised to 8.7:1 and a Dura-Spark ignition system was fitted. These modifications boosted horsepower and torque very slightly but, more importantly, they reduced fuel consumption. Owners were delighted to discover that they could squeeze an extra three miles from every gallon. Meanwhile, the Lima four-cylinder engine gained 3.5bhp through tuning improvements, rising to 91.5bhp at 5,000 rpm, and was partnered with a 3.44:1 axle ratio. The V6 Capris switched from the 3.09 axle ratio to a 3.22.

TIME OUT

Sadly, and despite the improvements (and the fact that it was an exceptionally good and well-liked car), the Capri's days in the US were numbered; 1977 was the final year of sale and imports of Capris had actually been stopped in the summer of that year. The remaining stock, 4,079 in total, took quite some time to sell. Some dealers would still be trying to move 1977 cars in 1978, although all would be registered as 1978 cars.

There were a number of reasons for the Capri's demise. Inflation had rocketed, the dollar had slumped in value, and the car became increasingly expensive to import. Once upon a time it had been a value-for-money car, but not any more. It's true that shifting production to Cologne made practical and economic sense for every market apart from the North American one; and, yes, the strength of the Deutschmark against the dollar didn't help profits, but other manufacturers managed to cope. Even any forthcoming emission issues could have been overcome by the simple (albeit relatively

↓ Roger Chastain's S/3, restored and owned by Team Blitz. (Team Blitz)

← Late-model Capri II 2.8. (Ford Motor Company)

expensive at the time) expedient of fuel injection. Fuel-injection technology was improving all the time and would soon be the only way that engines would meet emission requirements. However, what probably sealed the Capri's fate in America was the Mustang II (and the imminent arrival of the third-generation Mustang and its badge-engineered Mercury stablemate).

Although not one of the finest cars to emerge from the Ford stable, the Mustang II sold well. It got its V8 back in 1975 (but only after howls of protest by Mustang purists and Ford Marketing). The Mustang II saved the Ford brand during the dark regulatory years of the mid-1970s when there was an insurance crisis over muscle cars, an oil crisis over supply, and a government-mandated emissions compliance crisis in Detroit. Had the Mustang brand folded, then Ford would most likely have folded as well, and the same holds true today with the current Mustang.

Of course, the Capri II was a much better car than the Mustang II and there was every likelihood that the Capri III would triumph over the soon to be introduced third-generation Mustang. Enthusiasts who placed driving pleasure above

patriotism knew this, so did the motoring press, and so too did Ford. And there's the rub. Ford of America was not going to let the Capri continue to bloody the Mustang's nose.

This was corporate vanity as, in reality, the company's ethos wasn't quite as global as it professed to be. Publicly, Ford displayed much support for the Capri. However, behind closed doors and in the boardrooms the story was quite different. The fact that the Capri was doing so well was acceptable. What was not acceptable was that the Capri was highlighting the shortcomings of Ford of America's 'indigenous' sporting car, the Mustang II. For Ford's hierarchy this was proving to be a bitter pill to swallow.

It was patently obvious that Ford didn't want Mercury selling the European Capri against the home-grown Mustang (and the Mercury-badged Mustang when it arrived). The Capri had become a victim of its own success. Cologne stopped making US-specification Capris in August 1977 and that was effectively the end of the Capri in the US.

The Mustang, on the other hand, was in for the long haul. Not only did it manage to ride out this stormy and often turbulent period, but little by little it returned to its roots. With some of its styling cues taken from the 1969 Mustang, the latest iteration (a very good car indeed) offers a real connection with the past, whilst being very much a car of the present.

DNA TURNAROUND

However, and before too many accolades are heaped upon the latest generation Mustang it is important to highlight the connectivity that the Mustang brand has with the Capri. From 1974 through to the present day, it's not been a case of what the Mustang did for the Capri; it's actually more what the Capri did for the Mustang. The Mustang transferred some of its DNA to the original Capri. That's an irrefutable fact. But also irrefutable, although not widely publicised, is the fact that the Capri II actually transferred some of its DNA back to the Mustang.

The Mustang II, which came on line in 1974 and replaced the oversized Mustang of 1971–73, was based on the same chassis and platform as Ford's lacklustre but volume-selling Pinto. Stylistically it echoed the original Mustang, and had been scaled down to a more practical size; but it was essentially a Pinto with different bodywork. This isn't widely known. Even less well known is how the Mustang II and the Capri II are linked.

How? Well, the Mustang received rack and pinion steering for the first time in its history with the advent of the Mustang II (using a rack similar to the Capri Burman-designed rack). And what was the biggest and most powerful engine you could get in a 1974 Mustang? The Capri's Cologne 2.8L. The 1974 Mustang was the first (and only) year of the Mustang with no V8 option. The Capri V6 was 'the' big engine for the OPEC oil crisis. The Mustang II actually shared two of the Capri II's power plants, the other being the 2.3-litre 'Lima' 4.

Neither provided the Mustang with scintillating performance. Indeed, if a Capri 1600 were to indulge in a spot of drag-racing against a 2.8-litre Mustang II Mach I, at the quarter-mile point the Capri would be just one second adrift of the Mustang. Away from the drag strip, and into the curves, a well-driven Capri could see off a 2.8-litre Mustang II, much to the chagrin

↓ **The actual 700bhp 1.7-litre BDT as originally fitted to the Zakspeed 'Capri' Mustang. Now owned by Team Blitz. (Team Blitz)**

of its driver (and Ford of America). Even the introduction of the Mustang V8 with its 302cu in (4,949cc) emission-controlled engine only brought about a modest improvement. Why? Well, it only had a measly 129bhp, which works out at less than 30bhp per litre!

The four-speed manual transmissions for the Mustang II (and the Pinto) were European variants of the Capri. DNA transferred back to Mustang again. Even the PCD of the front hubs and back axles were, for the first time in Mustang history, borrowed from the Capri. Plus the Pinto, and thus the Mustang II, both had Rostyle wheels in the options list. The Mustang II even used carburettors that had already appeared on the Capri (the Holley-licensed Weber 5200 and the Weber DFAV).

Then, in 1980, some ten years after the Total Performance programme was killed off by Henry Ford II, he decided to restart Ford factory racing one more time in the USA and Canada. As a result, the Capri/Mustang link continued. In one of his final acts before stepping down as chairman, Henry Ford II decided that Walter Hayes should

return to the USA and once again repeat the magic he had conjured a decade earlier. To start the new racing Ford SVO (Special Vehicle Operations) department in the USA, Walter Hayes elected to bring with him another blast from the Capri's past, Michael Kranefuss. Kranefuss, the former head of the Cologne competition department (and Ford of Europe's motorsports director), had cut his organisational teeth running the highly successful Cologne Capri racing operation and overseeing Zakspeed's successful Capri racing programme. So, in a rather nice about turn, the two men selected to restore Mustang racing were effectively two men who were not only passionate about Capris, but were instrumental in the model's development and success!

And the very first vehicle that Hayes and Kranefuss put on to an American racetrack was a 1981 Zakspeed Capri that had been thinly disguised as a Mustang, complete with a BDT 1.7L Kent-derived motor delivering nearly 700HP in IMSA specification. So it was a Ford Capri (in disguise) that rekindled Ford's American racing programme. What's more, it was driven by

↓ **The X-Pack triple Weber kit.** **(David Morgan Jones)**

Ford Capri Series-X options

- Weber DFI5 carburettor
- Triple Weber 42 DCNF carburettors and special air filter
- Group I head gaskets
- Larger inlet and exhaust valves
- Cast alloy inlet manifold
- Special exhaust system
- Electric fuel pump

- Electronic ignition
- High-capacity radiator
- Limited slip differential
- Ventilated front disc brakes with Granada calipers
- 7.5in four-spoke alloy wheels
- 205/60/13 or 225/60/13 Pirelli P7 tyres

- Stiffened and shortened front springs (up 38% to 145lb)
- Gas-filled dampers (as fitted to the Capri RS3100)
- Uprated front anti-roll bar
- Anti-dive kit
- Glassfibre wheelarch extensions
- Rear spoiler

former Capri racer Klaus Ludwig on weekends when he wasn't busy winning the German DTM championship with his Zakspeed Capris back home. The Capri had come full circle.

The Capri II in New Zealand

Despite the new National Government's decision to reintroduce import duty etc, New Zealand was extremely loyal to the Capri. The punitive costs meant that Ford of New Zealand was forced to discontinue official Capri imports, but a large number of Ford dealers took it upon themselves to import Capris from the UK, and then from Germany when UK production ceased. The models tended to be Ghia and S variants.

The X-Files

Always at the forefront of marketing initiatives during the Capri II's swansong period, Ford introduced a new and very exciting scheme. Branded Series-X (although more commonly referred to as X-packs), Ford had cherry-picked components from the RS parts bible, sanctioned the production of a number of special body panels and enhancements, and marketed them in a range of kits, which could be fitted by Ford dealers. The range was impressive, with components being sourced from Ford AVO, Zakspeed, and other specialist companies. Fibresports, in Basildon, produced the fibreglass panels/spoiler etc.

Most of the modifications on offer could be applied to other Capri variants and there was nothing to stop you turning your 1300 Capri II into

a Series-X, although it was unlikely that anyone did. The conversion kits were aimed fairly and squarely at owners of the potent 3.0-litre models, the 3.0S in particular. See panel above for the very long list of options.

The engine components (triple Weber conversion) pushed the power of the V6 to 175bhp at 5,000rpm and the torque climbed to 194lb/ft at 4,000rpm. So equipped, a Capri could reach the benchmark 60mph in just 7.4 seconds. Flat out it would nudge 130mph. Of course, this supercar-slaying performance came at a cost. The complete kit was very expensive, fuel economy was appalling, and the triple-carburettors were a nightmare to tune, noisy, and often harsh.

Nevertheless, the X-pack truly transformed the Capri and made it a real fire-breather. When the famed motoring scribe L.J.K. Setright drove an X-packed Capri for *Car* magazine in 1980, he relished the experience: 'The cornering power seemed immense, traction fantastic; braking as good as the standard linings would permit. Driving the Capri was a revelation.'

Autocar also came away from its X-series road test impressed: 'As a fast and effortless car, the Series-X has numerous advantages. It can out-accelerate many cars with glamorous names, while spares and service are available everywhere.'

However, the writer did note that if you ordered a new Capri 3.0-litre at £6,252, and then instructed the dealer to fit the complete X-pack kit, you would not have had much change out of £10,000!

DID YOU KNOW?
Total Capri II production figure: 404,169. Production ended in March 1978.

CHAPTER 4
THE CAPRI III

The Capri III (which was never officially given this title – it just inherited it) was in reality an evolution of the Capri II. Ford gave the project the title Carla.

Initiated in April 1977, scheduled for March 1978, the new Capri actually arrived in the showrooms in April 1978. Even when one considers what Ford was capable of doing when it was pushed, a lead time of just ten months to update the Capri is quite remarkable. Apart from some minor details, and the retention of the 2.3-litre V6 Cologne for the German market, there were no real differences between UK and German Capri IIIs.

In addition to refreshing the Capri's appeal, the restyle was actually brought about for aerodynamic reasons too. The droop-snooted Capri concept car, the 'Modular Aerodynamic', which had been displayed at the 1976 Geneva Motor Show, provided strong visual clues of what was to come.

A melding of the Capri II, the Vauxhall Droopsnoot, the Vauxhall Sportshatch, and the Escort RS2000 Mk2, the 'Modular Aerodynamic' was a slippery customer indeed. Although the vaned grille, fared-in headlights, and flush wheeltrims didn't make it into production, the quad headlights and front and rear spoilers did. Surprisingly, the quad headlights improved the aerodynamics somewhat, but only because they were partly covered by the new bonnet line and wing edges. This, the lower bonnet line, and the new design of grille (which debuted on the Fiesta), all combined to help counteract the drag created by the front spoiler. Of course, greater downforce at the front almost invariably produces lift at the rear, so to pin the rear end to the ground Ford elected to fit an RS2000-style spoiler.

The Capri III certainly slipped through the air much more easily than its predecessor. Ford placed a great emphasis on this, and advertised the new Capri III as having a 0.403 drag factor. The S variants, with their lowered suspension, and body modifications, dipped below this and recorded 0.374.

There is no doubt that the revised aerodynamics improved economy. Ford had also tinkered with the engines to improve mpg and driveability. Fortunately for the UK and European markets, the engines weren't encumbered with too much in the way of emission control equipment, so the power outputs remained as before.

The most obvious change to the exterior was the addition of side rubbing strips on all except the S models. Practical, if rather utilitarian, the side stripes were mated to rather ungainly wraparound bumpers. The rear-light clusters had ballooned in size but at least they were aesthetically pleasing and sported a ridged pattern that shrugged off dirt. Unfortunately, the front indicators, previously housed in the front wings, were now positioned in the bumpers. So although the enlarged bumpers afforded the car more protection, in the event of a car park skirmish the indicators were likely to suffer adversely. The score was style 1, function 0. Oh … at long last a laminated windscreen was standardised across the range.

Ford had also been playing around with spring and damper settings (they did this almost from the start of Capri production through to the end) and fitted revised anti-roll bars, but the underpinnings were essentially much the same as before.

Value added

In addition to making their cars more appealing visually, Ford – in line with all other major car producers – was making its cars more attractive from a financial perspective too. The Capri's major service intervals were, for the most part, stretched from 6,000 to 12,000 miles (although the Essex V6's valve gear adjustment remained a 'must do' at 6,000).

← The new 2.8i went on sale in Germany first (in the background are a Capri 2.3S and a Capri 1300). (Ford Motor Company)

← Body and soul, the Tickford Capri pushed the styling and performance envelopes … and, as the advertising proudly boasted, it was 'One of the Fastest Cars in the World'. (John Colley Photography)

Quite how Ford managed to extend the service intervals is a bit of a mystery. The major mechanical components had not changed significantly. Perhaps some of Ford's claims were made with its corporate fingers crossed! In fairness, with almost a decade of Capri experience to draw on, Ford had a thorough knowledge of what usually went wrong, and after how long. The company had also strived to reduce running costs, and many items that were previously time-consuming to check (eg brake reservoir, battery level, washer bottle) could now be done at a glance, which made for a reduced labour bill at the dealers. What's more, structural and trim changes made the Capri much more repair-friendly and insurance costs reflected this. The Capri III was a premium car without the premium price.

IMPROVEMENTS, ADDITIONS, AND CHANGES

Having left things alone for a surprisingly long period, for the British market, Ford updated the interior specification in September 1978. The L gained a push-button MW/LW radio, whilst the Ghia was granted a slightly better system with

mono radio and a stereo cassette. However, even the best Ford audio system was far from being an audiophile's delight. Ford made very good cars, but for some reason it couldn't provide them with anything other than average audio systems.

More improvements followed in April 1979, which were minor but welcome. Depending on the model, these improvements centred on door mirrors, headlamp washers, and a 14in sports steering wheel similar in design to the RS2600 version. The S was treated to extra soundproofing, which made an already quiet car even quieter. Recaro seats were an option.

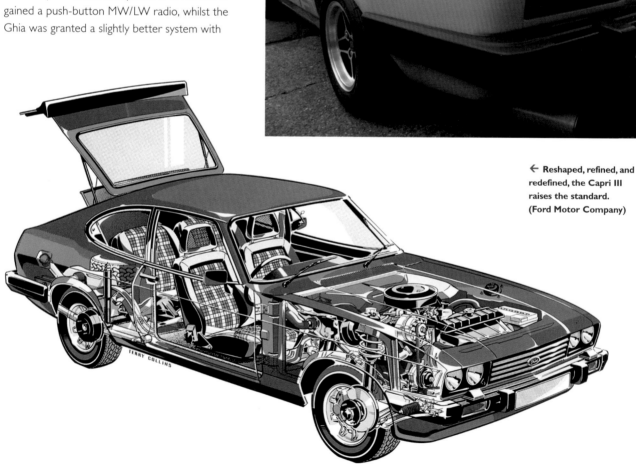

↓ **Wraparound bumpers and dirt-shrugging rear light clusters were all new. (David Morgan Jones)**

← **Reshaped, refined, and redefined, the Capri III raises the standard. (Ford Motor Company)**

As far as the engines were concerned, the
UK market bid a none too sad goodbye to the
50bhp 1300 and gave a lukewarm welcome to
the returning 57bhp version. The 1600 Pinto
delivered 72bhp in 1600L and GL guises, rising to
88bhp in the S thanks to a twin-choke Weber and
better manifolding. Power outputs for the 2.0-
litre GL, Ghia, and S, and the 3.0-litre Ghia and S,
remained unchanged and were 98bhp and 140bhp
respectively.

Oddly, in Germany (and in Italy and Sweden)
you could order your Capri with a 1300GT
engine, which delivered a healthy 73bhp. And
there was no 1300 option. Neither was there a
1600S option available in Germany, just the low-
compression 68bhp or high-compression 72bhp
versions. The 2.0-litre class was still catered
for, although, to confuse the issue, this could be
had as a 98bhp four-pot Pinto, or 90bhp six-
pot Cologne. A 108bhp 2.3-litre Cologne V6
was also available, but not the 2.8-litre. The top
engine was the 140bhp 3.0-litre Essex V6, but
it could only be had with the Ghia or S variants.
Confusing or what?

The X-Files

The X-series kits continued to be available. In line with the Capri's move towards becoming a more 'grown-up' coupe, the Capri III's X-series styling kits were much more subtle affairs. The arches now blended into the bodywork and continued much further up the front wings and rear three-quarter panels. Smooth!

With the appearance of Zakspeed's steroidal Group 5 racing Capris, Ford spotted a marketing opportunity and thus began an X-series push in Germany. The German X-series cars were badged as RS and could be ordered with Rallye Sport colour schemes. The body kits were the same as in the UK, but the engine options were significantly different.

Three tuning kits were offered. One was listed for the 1600 low-compression (taking power from 68 to 80bhp), another for the 1600 high-compression (72bhp to 88), the third being for the Essex V6 3.0-litre. These two modest upgrades for the 1600 seem rather odd, but it has to be remembered that the German type approval system (TÜV) was rather strict, and conversions were thoroughly vetted to meet all manner of requirements.

The upgrade for the V6 was even less involved and barely seemed worth the effort as it only delivered an extra 7bhp (taking the power to 145bhp). Interestingly, when the Essex V6 was first introduced in 1969 Ford was claiming that it produced 144bhp, which is only 1bhp shy of the German X-series upgrade ten years later!

In April 1980 the 1300, 1600, and 2.0-litre engines were equipped with a viscous fan in place of the mechanical one. Power, torque, and efficiency were slightly improved as a result. This modification was applied across the range and in all market areas. In Germany, the 2.3-litre V6 had been reinvigorated thanks to a slightly higher compression ratio, bigger valves, and better porting. With its grunty 114bhp (previously 108bhp), the lighter 2.3 could almost snap at the 3.0-litre's heels.

Gearboxes were the same in Germany as they were in Britain. The 1300 and the 3.0-litre, the polar opposites of the Capri range, had different gearboxes, but the rest of the range had the same unit, albeit with different ratios.

To help keep promoting the message that the Capri was indeed a sporting car, all benefited from gas-filled rear dampers (with the exception of the poverty-specification models). The S versions were blessed with Bilstein gas dampers, stiffer springing, and thicker anti-roll bars front and rear. These improvements made the Capri a truly sporting drive and enabled it to close the gap on its rivals. Surprisingly, the braking system remained as before, although Ford's engineers had been experimenting with various pad compounds.

Special editions

One way to make the familiar look less familiar, and hopefully more attractive, and thus boost sales, was to dress it up as a special edition. Ford was a past master of this type of marketing. A rash of special edition Capris was introduced. One appeared late in 1979 (it was a February 1980 introduction for the UK) and the other three arrived in July 1981.

The first was the GT4, based on the 1600L. This featured a six-clock dashboard with red highlights to the clocks themselves, and three-tone striping along the sides and across the bonnet. Although some way removed from a sporting Capri, it had the uprated suspension, carried a sporty tag, and was advertised with a definite sporting bias. Strong links were made to the Zakspeed Group 5 racers. The special GT4 option pack, which included head restraints, remote-control driver's door mirror, passenger door mirror, tailgate wash/wipe, and rear package tray, retailed at £149.99. A twin-choke carburettor was a £59.10 option. Available in three colours – Diamond White (£4,328), Strato Silver (£4,415), and Signal Red 80 (£4,367) – the GT4 is one of the rarest Capri variants, being a limited run of 500 in the UK with a similar number being produced for the European market.

It was followed by the jauntily monikered Calypso and Cameo models. The Calypso, which retailed at £5,120, was a two-tone beauty based on the 1600LS. The Cameo, based on the 1300L or 1600L and priced from £3,995, was aimed squarely at the budget market and came minus the centre console and side mouldings (which actually made for very clean lines). In addition to the Calypso and Cameo, there have been a number of references made to there being a Capri Tempo. However,

the Capri community is still waiting to see such a model in the flesh!

Not content with launching three special editions in such a short space of time, Ford went and introduced yet another. This was the Cabaret, which took to the stage in May 1982. Based on the Capri L, it was a curious mix of parts as it had two-tone paintwork, sports wheels, Ghia centre console, extra gauges, and tinted windows. Available with either a 1600 or 2.0-litre engine, it was slightly updated in December 1982 and became the Cabaret II. The Calypso had a similar makeover and became the Calypso II. Quite what the owners of the original Cabaret and Calypso felt about these updates is probably unprintable.

↓ **Not really a sporting Capri but with its stripes it certainly looked like one, and the advertising message definitely was! (Ford Motor Company)**

↓ ↓ **Flying the flag – the American flag. A nicely liveried X-Series 3.0S pace car at Brands Hatch. (Ford Motor Company)**

↑ ↑ **The Cabaret comes under the spotlight. (Ford Motor Company)**

↑ **The Laser – a leading light in what was now a much-reduced Capri range. (Ford Motor Company)**

Ford was obviously happy to flood the market with special editions, as in January 1984 the Laser arrived. This was based on the 1600L and would be followed in June by a slightly revised and mainstream Laser. Lasers boasted a colour-coded grille, headlamp surrounds, door mirrors, uprated suspension, meaty 185/70/13 tyres, funky four-spoke alloys, tinted glass, new cloth trim, a leather gear knob, radio/cassette, comprehensive instrumentation, five-speed gearboxes, and Laser motifs and decaling. The 1600 Laser retailed at £5,990. With the 2.0-litre engine the price rose to £6,371, but automatic transmission was a no-cost option on the 2.0-litre. The Laser was a very good concept and a very good car that did much to revive interest in the Capri. As did the 2.8i.

The Capri 2.8i – a new injection of life

Although the 3.0-litre Essex V6 had plenty of power and torque, and was a very good engine, it was a bit of a heavy breather. As the 1980s approached, Ford's engineers were patently aware of the fact that it wasn't going to breeze through the increasingly stringent emission regulations. In 1981, having run with this charismatic and hard-working engine for the best part of 22 years, Ford decided that it was time to say goodbye Essex and hello Cologne. It was also goodbye carburettor and hello fuel injection.

Ford had already had plenty of experience with the injected and highly specialist RS2600 and, in the late 1970s, a number of other injected Cologne-engined prototypes had been tested and with very favourable results. There was another reason for having to oust the Essex V6 … production logistics. With so many cars already sporting the Cologne V6, and with other applications in the pipeline, it made better sense to focus on this engine.

Ford's Special Vehicle Engineering (SVE) operation, under the direction of Rod Mansfield, had recently been set up in Dunton, Essex, and was given the job of developing a new, range-topping, Cologne V6-powered model. This was actually SVE's first project. The 2.8-litre Cologne engine had already found its way under the bonnet of American Capris and the Granada, but only in carburetted form. SVE got creative. Off came the carburettor and on went Bosch K-Jetronic fuel injection (a slightly different Bosch system was used for some markets). SVE then added an oil/water heat exchanger, large-bore, twin-pipe exhaust system, a viscous-coupled fan, changed the thermostat, strengthened the crankshaft, and fitted an improved radiator.

Thanks to these modifications the engine produced a creamy 160bhp. Even those steeped in Essex tradition had to concede that the Cologne V6 was much more refined and efficient. The only trade-off was a reduction in torque. Whereas the good old Essex thumped out 174ft/lb of torque at 3,000rpm, the Cologne V6 could only muster 162ft/lb at a heady 4,300rpm. Rev-limited to 6,300rpm, the 2.8i could hit 60mph in just 7.6 seconds and would just exceed 130mph flat out. As a bonus, the mpg was significantly better than the 3.0-litre Essex.

Of course, there was more to the 2.8i than just its engine. SVE had also been busy on the Capri's suspension and brakes. Riding an inch lower than its stablemates, with Bilsteins all round, stiffened (single-leaf at the rear) springs, larger diameter anti-roll bars front and rear, 7 x 13in Wolfrace

Sonic alloys, and 205/60/VR13 tyres, it not only looked as if it could devour corners, it did!

And, at last, here was a Capri with decent stoppers. Up front there were 9.76in ventilated discs and performance pads. The rear drums remained, but these had been equipped with harder linings. The so-called 'G-valve' helped apportion the braking loads when and where needed.

The styling and trim also came in for serious attention, making the 2.8i the most sporty looking and luxurious Capri yet seen. Externally, you could have solid, two-tone, or metallic paint, and all cars came with the all-important 'injection' wording on the front wings and rear hatch. Fuel-injection was quite something in the early 1980s and Ford wanted people to know about it! The mirrors were colour-coded, twin coachlines were applied, and a tilt and slide steel sunroof was standard.

On the inside the changes were almost as noticeable. Not only did you get Recaro seats, you also got Ford's finest crushed velour trimming in the appropriately named 'Carla' tartan. The door panels were similarly trimmed. In-car entertainment was never a Ford strongpoint, although the 2.8i benefited from a push-button stereo radio/cassette.

The German market was treated to the new Capri 2.8i first. Launched in March 1981 at the Geneva Motor Show, the 2.8i was approximately 17% more expensive than the outgoing 3000 Ghia. British enthusiasts had to wait until June 1981, when they could get their hands on a 2.8i for £7,995. Not only had the Capri come of age, it was a genuine high-performance car and something of a bargain too.

Popular Motoring's John Pearson pitched a Capri 2.8i against a 2.0-litre Audi Coupe. Despite being genetically linked to the fearsome and all-conquering Quattro, the Audi Coupe actually came second best to the revitalised Capri:

'Both are good performance cars with driver appeal as opposed to everyday humdrum transport.

'The modern designed Audi has more than adequate performance, good economy, and handling.

'Pity we matched it against the Capri which offers such a tremendous package for the price. Just over £8,000 isn't cheap, but in terms of what it offers compared with other more expensive cars then it's excellent value for money.'

↓ **A number of the UK's police forces also fell for the Capri 2.8i's charms and ability. (Ford Motor Company)**

Injection special

Ford was seemingly preoccupied with the Capri, which underwent a vast number of mechanical and cosmetic changes over the years. Even the 2.8i, which was pretty much perfect when it left the production line, barely reached its third birthday before it too was updated and improved.

April 1984 marked the German launch of the 2.8 Super Injection, which superseded the 2.8i. This new variant gained stylish seven-spoke RS alloys (but minus the RS script on the centre cap, as it wasn't an RS), leather-edged Recaros, leather steering wheel, leather-trimmed gear knob and door panels, body-coloured grille and headlight surrounds, and a Salisbury LSD. Britain got this new Capri in September, although for the home market the name had been changed to 'Injection Special'.

Surprisingly, having gone to so much trouble, production of the LHD Super Injection ceased in November, which meant that Britain was the sole recipient of the mechanically similar but differently monikered Capri. LHD Capri production would actually finish at the end of 1984, and with good reason. Fewer than 28,000 Capris were produced in 1983 and of these over 22,000 were RHD and made their way to the UK.

Understandably, as the Capri was in the twilight of its life, sales did begin to tail off, and it was coming under attack from the opposition and from Ford itself. The Escort XR3 and XR3i had undoubtedly stolen some sales from the Capri. However, there still remained a hard core of Capri cognoscenti who recognised a bargain when they saw one and a sizeable number were sold. On sale at £9,500, it was just £262 dearer than the 2.8i, but that £282 got you a lot of goodies. The Injection Special even came with a ZF LSD as standard.

The arrival of the Injection Special did much to rekindle the Capri's fire. In fact, for a while, the more traditionally styled Injection Special outsold the new 'jelly mould' Sierra XR4i by three to one.

Capri 280 – the not so limited edition

When Cologne began to wind up production of the Capri at the tail end of 1986, Ford reckoned that it had 500 bodyshells in stock. Accordingly, a plan was drawn up to produce a special run-out model called the Capri 500. Fortunately, before production commenced someone went and had a count up. You can imagine his or her (and Ford's) surprise when the tally went past the 500 mark and continued all the way to 1,038. Yes, that's correct, Ford had miscalculated. There were actually 1,038 bodyshells in stock, not 500. So, the special batch of '500' decals ended up in the bin, and Ford promptly decided to rename the car the 280 (well, Capri 1038 doesn't quite have the same ring about it does it?).

As far as can be ascertained, three 280s were actually registered new as automatics. The cars were manufactured as five-speed manuals then sent to a specialist company (thought to be in the Boreham area), where they were fitted with a four-speed Scorpio automatic gearbox. The conversion work was provided with a Ford warranty. One of the three cars was fitted with a Turbo Technics conversion; the other two had standard engines.

The 280 was and is a very desirable car. In many ways it is the ultimate roadgoing Capri. A good-looker, the colour scheme extended to the front grille, the red and white coachlines added a touch of class and incorporated 280 logos, and the glorious RS seven-spoke alloy wheels, now some 15in in diameter, were dressed with 195/50 low-profiles. Although essentially the same as a 2.8i Special, the interior benefited from full raven black leather trim complete with red piping.

Back in 1987 the 280 retailed at £11,999. What impacted most on 280 sales, of course, was the 2.8 Injection Special, which could usually be had with a sizeable discount. Because of this, many 280s would languish in the showrooms. Some were sold long after their actual date of manufacture. Had they sold as expected, all should have sported a 'D' prefix on their registration. They didn't, which explains why there are numerous E, F, and G registration 280s. Apparently there are three 280s in private ownership that are unregistered.

Most 280s are genuine. Nevertheless, there are likely to be a few fakes lurking amongst the classifieds. How do you spot a genuine one? Well, all were built during December 1986, and not one 280 was registered before 1987. The colour code on the VIN plate must state T7. The chassis numbers must begin 'GG' and have five numbers after that. If not, it's not!

← Fine-looking and fast – the RS2800T. (John Colley Photography)

The Capri 280 holds the accolade of being the last Capri to roll off the production line. The date? 19 December 1986.

The Capri III in New Zealand

Although still hamstrung by import duties and tariffs, Ford of New Zealand took it upon itself to import a number of Capri III models. The locally produced Cortina was the best-selling car in New Zealand, so having Capris in the showrooms kind of made sense. Not that the price made sense. For example, the Capri 2.8i ended up being twice the price of a Cortina. Some Ford dealerships also imported Capris, and a number of enterprising individuals managed to import some too. Capris were finding their way to New Zealand right until the end of production, and this included a number of Capri 280s.

The Turbocharged Capris

ZAKSPEED RS2800T

It may have been based on the standard Capri 2.8 Injection, but the Ford Capri RS2800T was anything but standard. Built to celebrate the success of Zakspeed's 1.4- and 1.7-litre turbocharged Group 5 Capri 'silhouette' racers in the DRM (Deutsche Rennsport Meisterschaft) series, it was quite a machine. There is some confusion over just how many were produced. A figure of 400 has been cited, but the number is ... to 200. What is certain is that all

were LHD, and all were built as part of the Ford Motorsport Performance Vehicles programme. Officially only available in Germany and Switzerland (although it would be offered to other European countries and two examples found homes in the UK), and only sold through German RS dealers, the buying process could be quite convoluted. Nevertheless, those enthusiasts who decided to opt for a RS2800T and hang in there were on to a good thing.

The RS2800T was a thoroughly sorted and exciting car that was even greater than the sum of its well-engineered and carefully selected parts. Despite its specialist nature, it was in fact an official Ford factory vehicle. And, contrary to what has often been said or indeed written, the RS2800T

↑ Engineered to perfection, the Zakspeed Capri's turbocharged Cologne V6. (John Colley Photography)

holds the honour of being the first turbocharged production car ever officially offered by Ford.

The turbo installation was largely the work of Michael May. Stuttgart-born May had shown great promise as an F1 driver, and had previously raced successfully in Formula Junior. However, a bad practice crash at the Nürburgring persuaded him to pursue his original vocation as an engineer. He not only worked on fuel injection development with both Porsche (for whom he was also a test driver) and Ferrari, he was also the first person to improve cornering speeds through the use of downforce. May also developed and raced a turbocharged Capri in 1969. Following this, he developed an Eberspächer/Bosch turbo installation for the 2.3 V6, which was rev-limited to 180bhp. This kit was actually homologated and it came with suspension and brake upgrades. Minus the limiter it could deliver 240bhp, and a competition-inspired 250bhp was also offered.

The Capri RS2800T was never a planned-for model, it sort of came about. Apparently, in 1979 Berkenkamp – a prominent German Ford dealership (which was a major player in motorsports) – offered a number of conversions using kits developed by Michael May. The cars converted were the Taunus, Granada, and Capri. The Capri was tested by several German magazines, which were enthusiastic about the results; they achieved 0–100kph in 7.4 seconds and a top speed of 131mph/211kph. Conversions were available for the 2.3 and 2.8 engines, with power outputs that ranged from 115 to 200bhp. The Berkenkamp Capri caught the attention of Ford and its German Motorsport division and the Capri RS2800T was given the green light.

Ford put an inordinate amount of effort into this project and from the outset reliability was paramount. In fact, Ford originally planned to fit a 2.8-litre Turbo engine into the Granada and then adopt a similar installation for the RS2800T, but reliability problems cropped up. Subsequently a plan was made to switch to a 2.3-litre Turbo engine for the Capri and a development programme was started. Having done so, Ford was soon in possession of a very driveable and reliable 150bhp car (up from the standard 2.3-litre car's 108bhp but some way down from the Berkenkamp/May kits). This level of power wouldn't have been a problem had it not been for the fact that Ford had recently released the Capri 2.8 Injection (Super Injection in Germany), which had 160bhp at its disposal. If the Zakspeed Capri was going to proceed, the powers that be decided that the project should revert to a turbocharged 2.8 V6 instead. Fortunately, in the interim, the 2.8-litre's reliability problems were overcome and the Capri did end up with the Granada PY-based 2.8-litre turbo engine.

The engine benefited from a H/P

tuftrided crank, higher quality valves, H/D head gasket, BEHR oil cooler, uprated oil lines, hoses and cooling components. The Garrett T4 turbo, which could run to a maximum 5.4lb of boost and sat on a special manifold, helped raise the power to 188bhp at 5,500rpm (67bhp/litre). Not a huge amount admittedly, but this engine's *raison d'être* was flexibility and driveability. The subtle turbo installation and thoughtful engineering meant that a very useful 201ft/lb of torque was available at 4,500rpm.

Contemporary road tests revealed that the RS2800T's mid- and top-end pulling power was awesome. It could reach the benchmark 60mph in just 7.7 seconds, and with pedal to the metal in fourth the needle was hovering above the 140mph mark.

To separate it from the rest of the Capri range, the RS2800T boasted a dramatic external appearance. The flared front and rear wings from the Series-X range were fitted, as was an extremely purposeful and effective large double rear wing. The double wing produced so much downforce that the German authorities insisted that the car be fitted with a front spoiler to prevent the front lifting at speed on the autobahns. Building it without the front spoiler was *verboten*! Naturally, the design of the front spoiler echoed that of the Group 5 Zakspeed racing Capris.

Sold exclusively through RS dealers, the RS2800T's price in Germany represented a modest 10% premium over that of a 2.8 Super Injection. For that measly price increase you got a whole lot of extras and a heck of a lot of street cred. Available in a variety of colours, the most popular proved to be red, silver, and white. The all-important 'turbo' badges were penned in an italic script and applied to the bonnet, the tailgate, and the doors. Based on a Capri 2.3S the RS2800T featured a standard Injection/Ghia grey interior except for the substitution of Scheel front seats. These carried small RS badges and were identical to the type fitted to the Escort RS1600i of the same era. Trimmed in grey velour and with matching retrimmed rear seats and Injection door trims, the interior was rather classy … in a sporting kind of way.

Equipped with impressively wide (for the period) 235/60/13 tyres, mounted on delectable and wide for the period 7½ x 13in RS alloys, the RS2800T stuck like glue – on smooth tarmac … and in the dry. When the road surface was less good, and/or wet, the RS2800T tended to let the driver know that it was a rear-wheel-drive car. And although the RS2800T used the Series-X brakes these were not as effective or as good as those fitted to the 2.8 Injection. Apparently the brakes were always considered to be the car's weak point.

The only options were a 75% limited slip differential and, where regulations demanded it, an optional smaller tyre was available for snow chains, mounted on a plain 6.5in-wide steel wheel.

Intended to be as cost- and time-effective as possible, the build was actually quite an expensive and convoluted process. The cars were built as a Capri 2.3S on the main line then moved to a smaller facility to have the engines fitted. The bodyshells were then sent to Zakspeed at Neiderzissen, where the glassfibre X-series body panels were fitted. When the glassfibre work was completed and ready for painting, the shells would be returned to Cologne to be finished. All RS2800Ts had a unique build configuration.

Although not officially an RS, the RS2800T (sometimes called the 2.8T or RS2800 Turbo), thanks to its rarity, exceptional engineering, and motorsports inspiration, is welcomed by the RS Owners' Club.

TICKFORD 2.8T

It wasn't just the Germans who were getting all excited about turbocharging Capris; the UK market had long been in favour of forced induction. Lotus test driver, journalist, and Capri enthusiast John Miles was of the opinion that if properly developed a turbocharged Capri was, whilst remaining a very practical proposition, capable of reaching speeds in excess of 140mph and could have handling to match.

Following meetings with Victor Gauntlet (Chairman of Aston Martin) and Bob Lutz (Chairman of Ford Europe), the seed of his idea began to germinate. The aims were to produce a car that had the looks and performance of the Aston Martin Vantage but kept the practical advantages of the basic Capri. Things looked promising but, unfortunately, just as the project got under way Bob Lutz was promoted to a higher position within Ford of America. With Lutz out of the picture, the project was put on hold. Thankfully, and rather bravely, Miles and Gauntlet decided to continue, and an agreement was drawn up to manufacture 250 Tickford Turbos at the

Based on the 2.8i, the Tickford Capri 2.8T was every bit as special as it looked. The body kit (designed by Simon Saunders, chief designer, director, and owner of the Ariel Motor Company, which produces the awesome Ariel Atom) was unique to the Tickford Capri. With its colour-coded and blanked-off grille, deep front bumper, aggressively styled sideskirts with a ground-effect design at the rear, and wedge rear spoiler, it helped drop the drag coefficient to 0.37, and it was estimated that front- and rear-end lift had been reduced by 40%. The letterbox air intake, necessary to complete the aerodynamic package, proved to be a mixed blessing. Owners soon discovered that overheating could be an issue if the cooling system wasn't in A1 condition, and it was essential that the electric fan operated correctly. Although the interior was essentially from the 2.8i, Tickford dressed it with leather trimming, walnut veneer, a modified centre console, and electric windows. To deter miscreants from trying to obtain a 'free' Tickford an alarm was fitted. Options included deep-pile Wilton carpeting, a stainless steel exhaust, and full leather trim.

That was the show ... and, fortunately, the 2.8T had the go to match. Under the bonnet lurked a 2.8i Cologne V6 to which had been added an IHI turbocharger (mounted on a bespoke manifold), a Garrett intercooler, and AFT digital ignition. Power rose from 160 to 205bhp and torque was a massive 260ft/lb at just 3,500rpm. The all-important (as far as bar talk goes) 0–60mph was dispatched in a mere six seconds and the Tickford could nudge 140mph on a suitable road. In-gear acceleration was devastating, although contemporary road tests commented that the power arrived in an all-or-nothing fashion.

To cope with the Tickford's urgent power delivery, the rear end had been treated to an A-frame, the LSD remained (but the diff cover was now finned aluminium in place of plain steel), and the springs had been uprated. And, to ensure that the car stopped, the rear drums had made way for 10.43in solid discs. Despite the upgrading, the 2.8T was a bit of a beast. Car magazine's Roger Bell, who tested a 2.8T in 1983, noted that 'boost pressure peaks on full throttle, triggering turbo surge which borders on the violent – too violent in the wet'.

Although Bell had certain reservations, he came away from the road test impressed: 'All told, Tickford have done a thoroughly professional job in lifting the humble Capri to dynamic and luxury standards it's never reached before.'

↑ ↑ **Tickford's well-engineered turbo installation. (John Colley Photography)**

↑ **A bespoke interior: sumptuous leather, classy walnut veneer, and deep-pile Wilton carpeting. (John Colley Photography)**

Coventry plant where Jaguar's XJ-S cabriolets were finished.

The mechanicals were developed by Aston Martin, with assistance from SVE in Dunton. Although originally destined to be a regular production model, the Tickford Capri 2.8T (as it was called) was only a semi-official Ford model and sold through selected dealerships. You could have any colour you liked, as long as it was red, white, or black.

The Tickford 2.8T was a very fine car indeed … but there were two major issues. Firstly, there was the price. In 1982 a Capri 2.8i could be yours for £8,125, whereas the Tickford would relive you of a whopping £14,895! By 1986, although the specification had changed slightly, the price had risen to over £17,000. If you ticked all the option boxes, you'd have spent an extra £7,000 plus. As good as it was, you had to be utterly convinced of its virtues before forking out such a sum on a Capri.

Secondly, in 1986 Ford introduced the awesome Sierra Cosworth. This massively capable and charismatic car proved to be the Tickford's 'in-house' nemesis. The Sierra Cosworth was cheaper and faster than the 2.8T, although, to be fair, the two cars were very different propositions indeed.

Interestingly, Tickford had worked on a number of projects with Ford. So when Ford was looking to homologate the Sierra RS500, the company struck a deal with Tickford to produce 500 very special road cars. At the end of the run of Sierra RS Cosworths, Ford produced an additional 500 vehicles that were stored away. It was these cars that went to Tickford to be modified to RS500 specification.

Tickford's involvement wasn't quite as successful. The planned-for production run of 250 Tickford 2.8Ts never happened. In fact it is thought that

just 85 cars were sold. Tickford actually bought 100 2.8is – the remaining 15 cars were sold on as standard 2.8 injection specials, but they have Aston Martin Tickford VIN plates. Although not a huge success in its heyday, good 2.8Ts are now very much sought after.

Tailpiece

With the genes from the Mustang encoded within its DNA, the Capri was a rather special creation. A clever combination of sound engineering, accessibility, adaptability, aspirational appeal, overall ability, and sheer unadulterated style, the Capri excited imaginations over 40 years ago, and it's still exciting them today.

↓ **Body and soul, the Tickford Capri pushed the styling and performance envelopes … and, as the advertising proudly boasted, it was 'One of the Fastest Cars in the World'. (John Colley Photography)**

CHAPTER 5
THE RS CAPRIS

As we have seen, the RS designation (standing for 'Rallye Sport') was first applied to the iconic Escort RS1600, which, in 1970, was the first production car to receive the Cosworth BDA engine. In fact, the BDA engine was not officially planned for the Escort. The first car to receive a BDA transplant was actually a Cortina Mk2, and it was its impeccable performance and behaviour in the Cortina that did much to convince Ford that it should be united with the Escort, and that it should also be considered for the Capri.

The year 1970 was very important for the British arm of the Ford Motor Company. This was the year in which the Ford Advanced Vehicle Operations (AVO) was established in South Ockendon, Essex, and also when Ford's Rallye Sport dealer network was set up.

The relationship between AVO and the RS network was symbiotic. AVO's brief was to build performance versions of the Ford range of cars and manufacture tuning equipment. The Rallye Sport dealer network was charged with the task of merchandising the AVO products to the public. Not that AVO was solely involved with the high-performance market. From time to time it had to find other ways of paying the bills and wages. For a while it busied itself assembling thousands of Escort 1300Es!

The RS2600

It wasn't long after the RS1600 burst on to the performance car scene that the first of the RS Capris broke cover. Poised, purpose-built, and a real performer, this new Capri would tease and tempt enthusiasts, although, as has already been noted, its primary purpose was to enable Ford of Germany to go racing … properly.

To get the Capri approved for racing by the sport's governing body, the FIA, Ford needed to create an homologation special, a road-legal car that could be produced in the required quantity (50) and be similar, both in appearance and mechanically, to the version intended for racing. The car that Ford came up with was the highly desirable Capri RS2600.

Although Ford had been successful with Capris in competition, Jochen Neerpasch – Ford's competition chief in Germany – quickly realised that the company needed a pukka pure-bred Capri, one that was aimed fairly and squarely at circuit racing.

According to contemporary regulations for the class in which Ford intended to compete, cars had to weigh in at a minimum of 900kg and be powered by an engine that fitted within international class standards. This meant that the engine had to be around 2.6 litres but could be enlarged to almost 3.0 litres.

Having paved the way with the RS1600 and the Mexico, the small team at AVO, headed by Ray Horrocks and Bob Howe, was charged with the task of doing most of the development work on the Capri RS2600. Working to Neerpasch's brief, AVO began creating a Capri homologation special, the iconic and charismatic RS2600.

Approval had been granted for the project as early as November 1969 and the race was soon on. A fully dressed but dummy-engined RS2600 was displayed at Geneva in March 1970. By the following month, Ford's Pilot plant at Niehl (which is where Ford's pre-production cars and prototypes are built and checked) had managed to produce 50 cars in readiness for homologation. Although only around 20 were actually fully built, homologation for the RS2600 was duly granted in October 1970. Interestingly, these cars had the requisite long-stroke crankshaft (to enable them to be taken over 2.6 litres for competition) but were minus the injection system. Indeed, the injection wasn't actually required for competition purposes;

↑ **The RS2600, which would be successful on the racetracks and in the showroom. (Ford Motor Company)**

it was needed to deliver production model driveability on the road cars. So it's almost by default that the RS2600 actually holds the honour of being the first Ford production car to feature fuel injection.

The all-important first 50 cars were spartan, no-nonsense road-burners, and they entered the world almost naked. Minus carpets, soundproofing, a heater, etc, and with GRP doors, bonnet, and boot, Perspex sliding windows, thinner glass, fewer coats of paint, slim bucket seats, and genuine (and very expensive) Minilite magnesium wheels, these were raw and feral machines. All this was done to save weight, of course. Even so, the 'lightweight' Capris, or 'Plastikbombes', as they became known, still struggled to dip as low as 900kg. The RS2600 was approved with a minimum weight of 900kg for racing, although no competition Capri would ever be this anorexic. In reality 950kg was about the lowest weight ever recorded.

Getting the 50 cars ready in such a short time was an impressive feat. Also impressive was the amount of clever engineering work AVO had undertaken. AVO was brimful of talent – talent such as Richard Martin Hurst, Reg Chapman,

Graham Parker, John Hinds, Harry Worrall and, of course, Rod Mansfield. The initiative for the RS2600 may have come from Germany, but it was the guys at AVO who should take most of the credit for its creation.

Although the RS2600 Capri was homologated for Group 2 racing, what is sometimes overlooked is that the roadgoing RS2600 was a genuine and very useable production car. By the time production ended in 1974 (although one car was actually built in 1975), thousands had been built. Making a specialist car for competition purposes is one thing – making it into a suitable production vehicle, one that could pass quality control and TUV etc, is another.

The first production RS2600 rolled off Neihl's line on 14 September 1970 … or at least, it would have had it not been for the fact that, horror of horrors, the wheels were fouling! Because of revisions to the front cross-member – mainly to induce the right amount of negative camber (the holes for the TCAs were drilled in a different position to the standard car) – the 6in-wide Richard Grant alloys (the credit-busting magnesium Minilites only adorned the 50 'Plastikbombes') were coming into contact with their arches.

Thankfully, due to its very nature the Niehl factory was able to adapt to meet such challenges. Within a week its engineers had fabricated a simple tool that reshaped the front arches slightly, providing the necessary clearance as well as giving them their trademark appearance. Other RS2600 trademarks were the rectangular wing badges (same style as the MkI RS Escorts) reading 'RS2600', an RS roundel on the offside of the boot lid, and a bib spoiler (in either steel or GRP). The interior of the RS2600 was quite special too, with its cloth-covered Scheel seats (with adjustable backrests), dished Springalex steering wheel, and full V6 instrumentation, etc, but no centre console.

What was so impressive about the RS2600 was just how many of its components were taken directly from the competition department's shelves and the production line's parts bins. The RS2600 was a specialist car, but not a bespoke one. The front coil springs were stock competition department items, as were the rear single-leaf springs. Dampers came from Bilstein and the settings were the result of accumulated experience and testing. The RS2600 sat very low to the ground and was stiff-riding too. Brakes were stock 3.0-litre/2600GT items with anti-fade material provided by Ferodo. They were servo-assisted, although the 7in servo (German Capris were still running the smaller servo) wasn't overly efficient.

With its longer throw crankshaft, the 2.6-litre Cologne V6 had grown to 2,673cc and would later swell to 2,995cc for racing purposes. It was a potent unit, which was fitted with high-compression pistons and the perky camshaft from the 2300GT. The modifications resulted in a healthy 150bhp at 5,800rpm and 165ft/lb of torque at 3,500rpm. This meant that the RS2600 could rush from 0 to 62mph in just 8.6 seconds and, on the autobahns, a top speed of 124mph was available … for a while.

Initially, Ford chose to fit the RS2600 with the type of gearbox as found in the Taunus V6 range. With its 3.22:1 axle ratio (the tallest available at the time for the Capri) it was geared at just 20mph for every 1,000rpm – fine for rapid acceleration, but less than satisfactory for autobahn-storming. A number of owners soon discovered that continuous

↓ **RS2600 power: Ford's first production fuel-injected engine. (Ford Motor Company)**

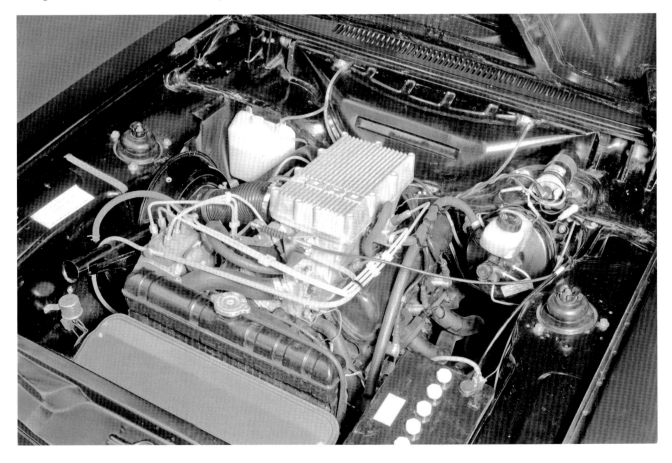

120mph-plus running usually ended in tears, and an autobahn strewn with the tortured remains of an overworked Cologne V6.

Much to the relief of subsequent owners (and the warranty department), in October 1971 the Taunus gearbox was replaced by a Granada unit, and a 3.09:1 axle ratio was installed, which allowed for nearly 22mph/1,000rpm, dropping the revs by almost 10% as a result. A new design of front hub and vented disc, unique to the RS2600, also found its way on to the car. So equipped, the RS2600 now had stopping power as well as staying power.

Externally, the RS2600 gained chrome quarter-bumpers all round (the fronts being home to the indicators), and the two vents in the front panel were deleted. Wheels were now the RS FAVO four-spoke items. The bodywork, as with the earlier cars (which could be ordered in Ford racing colours, ie silver and blue) was finished in the same style as the German Capri GTs, which meant that the bonnet, engine bay, wing tops, screen pillars, and tops of doors (fading out at the rear quarter-windows) would be Satin Black. Ford racing colours were an option, as were solid colours.

Inside, the Scheel reclining seats had been restyled and retrimmed in a softer cord material and had a small RS badge at the top of the backrest. The rear seats were now contoured, although only their inserts were trimmed.

The arrival of the facelifted Capri inevitably impacted on the RS2600, and it too underwent a facelift. Prior to this the RS2600 had not been overly adorned, but post-facelift it featured an enhanced decal set. This included one that edged the power bulge (with the word 'Injection' appearing either side of the bulge at the rear), a roundel on the fuel filler cap reading 'RS 2600 Injection', another in the same position on the nearside rear quarter, and one running along the lower boot edge. The decals were available in white, black, and blue. Bumpers were still quarter width at the front but full width at the rear and were now finished in black. The nearside front bumper iron incorporated a towing eye. Spot lamp brackets were also fitted up front and these helped support the quarter-bumpers. The headlamps became Hella units (previously Cibie) whilst bezels were GXL type (earlier models used the federal type), and wing badges were now the shield type and read '2600V6'.

Inside, the RS2600 had become almost too well specced for a homologation special. It had the flat three-spoke steering wheel, a centre console, and a map-reading lamp. The seats remained the same up front, but the contoured rears were now all cloth rather than just the insert panels.

Mechanically the Kugelfischer Injection was switched to the C1 pump (earlier cars used the B1 pump along with injectors that could be dismantled and rebuilt). Also new were different injectors, fuel lines, and the throttle body. Some of the pre-facelift cars were also fitted with the C1 pump.

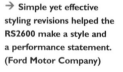
→ **Simple yet effective styling revisions helped the RS2600 make a style and a performance statement.** (Ford Motor Company)

The RS2600 sold very well. No doubt this was down to its raw ability, and the fact that there were a surprising number of options available, including a limited slip differential, opening rear quarter-windows, sunroof, radio, head restraints, and spot lamps. Whilst the RS2600 was never officially sold in Britain, over the years a few examples found homes here. It is thought that there are currently just a handful of RS2600s in the UK and these include the two that Ford converted to RHD – one for Walter Hayes, the other for Stuart Turner.

The contribution that the Capri RS2600 made to Ford, and to its success in European Touring Car Racing, cannot be underestimated. To many enthusiasts the RS2600 is the ultimate Capri.

The RS3100

In addition to developing the RS2600 as a racecar, Ford had been busy working on its replacement, the RS3100. The RS2600 had reached the end of its development by 1973 and was in desperate need of a fully-fledged aerodynamic package. As good as it was – and it was very, very good – the racing RS2600 was an extremely difficult creature to tame. BMW, Ford's nemesis in the European Touring Car Championship, had introduced the potent and bespoilered 3.0 CSL 'Batmobile', which, with its homologated and highly efficient aerodynamic aids, was well planted on the tarmac. Ford did its best with the RS2600, and attempted to homologate various aerodynamic appendages, but to no avail. The BMWs began to outstrip the Capris. At Spa they were lapping around eight

seconds faster than the quickest Capri.

What was needed, and quite urgently, was a new version of the Capri, one that would look superficially like the RS2600 but would be blessed with a completely different engine, numerous layout changes, and better aerodynamics. That car was the RS3100.

Approval for the RS3100 road car was given on 25 September 1973. The RS3100 was to be a limited volume Capri RS derivative that would be built at Halewood during November/December 1973. According to Ford it was to be 'based on the Capri 3000GT, but with an engine overbored to 3.1-litres, a front air dam and rear spoiler and with suspension, brakes and alloy road wheels carried over from the RS2600. Cars will only be sold through Rallye Sport dealers.'

Every modification that Ford sanctioned for the RS3100 was important, but there was one component that it needed more than any other: the famous ducktail spoiler. Like every other competition-orientated part on the car, the spoiler had been developed by AVO, which had carried out full aerodynamic tests in conjunction with MIRA (the Motor Industry Research Association). The ducktail, together with the front spoiler, enabled the RS3100 to record a drag factor of 0.375, which was the best figure ever recorded for a MkI Capri.

The RS3100, like the RS2600, was a proper production car. Unlike the RS2600, however, it had a very limited production run – RS2600 production outnumbered the RS3100 by a ratio of over 14 to 1. Only 250 RS3100 Capris were built, 249 at Halewood during November 1973, whilst the

other one was built at South Ockendon and was possibly one of the six pre-production cars. To gain its all-important Group 2 homologation, Ford needed to build 1,000 over the winter of 1973/74. This just didn't happen. Surprisingly, Henry Ford II had even signed off an RS2800 Capri. This didn't happen either, at the time, but the idea was later reincarnated as the Capri 2.8i.

With only 249 production versions to present to the FIA, Ford should have been rather stymied. However, the homologation process is a curious affair, which, over the years, has been open to interpretation. Many have mastered the art of homologation, and used it to their advantage, Ford included. By never releasing precise figures, and by ordering lots of parts to show that it 'intended' building more cars, Ford skilfully manoeuvred its way through the homologation process. Homologation was duly granted on 1 January 1974.

Based on the standard 3000GT, the RS3100 didn't have any optional extras, but there were small differences between individual cars. Some had red needles on the dashboard, others white (as on the Capri II), a number had imitation leather gear knobs, others had plastic, and a few were

fitted with inertia safety belts although most had static belts.

Mechanically the RS3100 sported an Essex 3.0-litre V6 bored out to 3,093cc with an inlet manifold and cylinder head ports that were hand polished, a re-jetted DGAS carburettor, and a slightly raised compression. Everything else was as standard with the exception of the rocker covers, which were always painted blue. The engine's output was 148bhp at 5,000rpm and it produced 187lb/ft of torque at 3,000rpm. A test engine had been trialled with a reprofiled camshaft and dual pipe exhaust system, which raised the power to 165bhp. In the end, however, it was decided to plump for driveability and stick with the lower power engine specification.

The suspension was almost, but not quite, as per the RS2600. This meant Bilstein shock absorbers all round (with revised valving), revised rear bump rubbers, and single-leaf springs with lowering blocks at the rear. Spring rates were slightly down on the RS2600 at 142lb front, 112lb rear. As on the RS2600, the front cross-member was also drilled to give negative camber. Brakes were pure RS2600 with its unique hub and vented disc assembly and Granada calipers. All the other components were stock 3.0-litre items.

For the interior Ford elected to go for a predominantly black theme, with black headlining and black PVC seats. All other fitments were as the standard 3000GT Capri.

RS3100s were available in seven different colours, which were: Diamond White, Daytona Yellow, Sebring Red, Modena Green, Stardust Silver, Olympic Blue, and Marine Blue. All were dressed with gold decals around the power bulge, around the rear of the car, and a triple line down the flanks. Externally the RS3100 also differed from the standard 3000GT, with quarter-bumpers up front (the nearside bumper iron incorporating a towing eye) along with a steel bib spoiler and a pair of spot-lamp brackets, which helped support the bumpers (no spot lamps were fitted), and a single-piece rear bumper finished in black. The flared front wings were as per the RS2600, but the 6 x 13in RS alloys were the same design and type as fitted to the 1973 model year RS2600. To check the wheels for authenticity, these are the only RS wheels that have 'Capri' and '73' cast into their reverse side.

The ducktail spoiler, which only arrived with the RS3100, was an impressive-looking affair. Vital too, being essential in keeping the rear end of the racing Capris pinned to the ground. If only such an item had been homologated for the RS2600!

If you wanted an RS3100 you could only obtain one through the RS dealership. Sadly, however, not many people wanted an RS3100. There were three major issues that prevented it from being the sales success it so deserved to be.

Firstly, in October 1973 the oil crisis erupted. Understandably people began to covet economy and not performance. Despite the obvious appeal, and having generated a good deal of interest, most RS3100s languished in the showrooms.

Secondly, by expending so much effort on what was an obsolete model, Ford had shot itself in its marketing foot. However good the RS3100 was, and it was good, there was no disguising the fact that it was the 'old' shape. Not that Ford had any option other than to use the Mk1 as the basis for the RS3100 road and race programme … it was the only version available at the time. The company had to get out on track and it had to win.

Last but not least was the cost. At £2,450 the RS3100 was not a budget model, although huge discounts were on offer.

Some were used as management lease cars and 23 were given to area sales managers in an attempt to stimulate interest. Even so, it was ages before all found homes. In a desperate attempt to clear stocks, 50 were exported to Australia during June and July 1974.

The slow take-up was a glitch, a major glitch. Nevertheless, it wasn't long before the RS3100 began to appreciate in value and gain the status it deserved. For some time now, good examples have been hugely sought after and commanded premium prices. Even basket cases fetch serious money. The RS3100 is a coveted classic.

Even though the RS3100 was not a commercial success in its heyday, it was and is a superb car. At the time it was also the fastest Ford production car thanks to its lusty engine, which propelled the RS3100 from 0 to 60mph in approximately 7.6 seconds and on to a top speed of 125mph. Like the RS2600, the RS3100 has racing blood coursing through its veins and a heritage to be proud of.

↓ **Jackie Stewart shows off his latest hairstyle, the Ford rally jacket, and the RS3100's all-important 'ducktail' spoiler. (Ford Motor Company)**

DID YOU KNOW?
Total Capri **RS2600** production figure: 3,532.

Total Capri **RS3100** production figure: 249.

CHAPTER 6
THE CAPRI IN MOTORSPORT

It was always mooted that the Capri should try its hand at motorsport and this proved to be the case, as both Ford of Britain and Ford of Germany would take the Capri under their competition wings. Despite some differences in their aims as well as their managerial style, both would extract the very best from the Capri.

Ford of Germany had already established a competition department at Cologne in 1968, which, as we have seen, was headed by Jochen Neerpasch, ably assisted by his deputy Mike Kranefuss and chief engineer Martin Braungart (who'd come from Mercedes Benz).

The decision to supplement the Boreham department with a similar operation in Cologne was made by Walter Hayes. Initially it was the intention for Cologne to handle its entire race and rally programme independently, but the two motorsport departments soon began working together and the gap between Cologne and Boreham became ever narrower. Lines of demarcation were certainly drawn, but the two departments did work exceptionally well together. Ford of Germany would be responsible for running most of the Capri's racing programme, with Ford of Europe handling the rallying exploits. The Capri was certainly instrumental in developing what would prove to be a generally harmonious and very successful motorsports partnership.

Capris in rallycross

Success sells. When the Escort was launched, Ford made sure that it was a winner. Indeed, an Escort had won its first ever competitive event, a rallycross, at Croft, a feat that the Capri would replicate when Roger Clark slithered his Capri to a worthy win at Croft in February 1969. This was actually the Capri's competition debut, on 8 February 1969 to be exact. Roger Clark took the win in front of the ITV's *World of Sport* cameras (he would go on to win the ITV/Castrol-sponsored series in the Capri), but he had to work hard. Four-wheel-drive Capris were born to understeer. Even when fully developed their natural trait was to push the nose wide. Nevertheless, a win's a win, and this particular one was timed to perfection, as it came only three days after the Capri had been launched.

Rallycross was a huge draw in the late 1960s and early 1970s. Indeed, it was so popular that the BBC used to televise the Castrol-sponsored series. An audience of five million was almost guaranteed (BBC's *Top Gear* programme is currently drawing an audience of around seven to seven and a half million).

Even though this was over a decade before Audi had shown other manufacturers the way forward with its all-conquering (for a time) Ur quattro, Ford's engineers appreciated that the only way a highly tuned 3.0-litre Capri was going to get its power down on a predominantly loose and slippery surface was if it had four-wheel drive.

The first two rallycross Capris were actually produced by Harry Ferguson Developments, a company well respected and well known for its pioneering work and expertise with four-wheel-drive technology. Jensen Motors had been working with Harry Ferguson Developments since 1962 to use the Ferguson Formula four-wheel-drive system on their cars, the development being slowed due to other projects. In 1966 Jensen released the world's first four-wheel-drive production car, the Jensen FF, featuring the Ferguson Formula four-wheel-drive system, which had been developed by Major Tony Rolt, Freddie Dixon, and Claude Hill, with funding from Harry Ferguson Developments. Rolt, who went on to establish Ferguson Formula Developments (FFD), had been imprisoned in Colditz castle during the Second World War and had also been awarded the Military Cross for gallantry. He died in 2008.

← An immaculately presented Kent Frami Racing 1972 Group 2 Capri RS2600. (Magic Car Pics)

In addition to Ferguson Developments, Ford's own engineers at Boreham would play a huge part in the project's evolution and success. This really was an undertaking that drew upon many talents, and from many quarters, and the scale of the engineering involved was enormous. The Capri had never been envisaged as a four-wheel-drive car and it showed – literally. A huge amount of metal had to be removed in order to fit the four-wheel-drive system: the bulkhead and scuttle had to be altered, and the chassis rails required serious surgery. All of this metalworking had to be undertaken before Mick Jones, who was Boreham's multi-talented workshop foreman, fabricated special subframes and so on. All in all the project was an incredibly complex one.

The fact that the Capri worked at all, points to the fact that the people involved were talented and versatile. Six rallycross Capris were built (four by Boreham), with power outputs ranging from

← The Capri's first ever competition win – Roger Clark at Croft in 1969. (Ford Motor Company)

→ Stan Clark at work. (Ford Motor Company)

212bhp to 250bhp (initially the engines were going to be BDA units, but these didn't have the sheer grunt needed). One was even fitted with automatic transmission and was occasionally driven by the very talented Barry Lee, who did a huge amount of the development test-driving. All had the differential-in-sump final drive for the front wheels, Ferguson Developments drive-transfer units, robust ZF gearboxes, and Ford Taunus front struts.

There is no doubt that this project was fraught with difficulties, yet it was ultimately successful and the lessons learnt were important ones.

→ The final incarnation of the rallycross Capri with mega-tuned Weslake V6, fuel injection, a serious set of rampipes, and flared arches. (Ford Motor Company)

↑ Piot on the 1969
Tour de Corse.
(Ford Motor Company)

As a pure PR exercise it most certainly succeeded. The various rallycross Capris that appeared over the next few seasons did wonders for Ford's image. The cars were successful too, although that success has to be attributed to the efficacy of the re-engineering and the skill of drivers of the calibre of Roger Clark, Stan Clark, Rod Chapman, and John Taylor, who did their utmost to counteract the cars' wayward handling characteristics. And they were very wayward! The traction was certainly impressive, but unless the cars were literally thrown into a corner, and set up with a controlled oversteer, they didn't handle. Driven normally, they'd reward the driver with terminal understeer and the inevitable 'off'. There were other inconveniences too, including driveshaft breakages, overheating, and various additional mechanical maladies. Nevertheless, when the four-wheel-drive Capris ran well, they usually won.

A spin-off (!) from the rallycross programme was that FFD produced 17 four-wheel-drive Capris. AVO had been heavily involved in this project too. A number of these were used for evaluation by the police and by Ford, the latter

having even considered putting the model into production. This never happened. The conversion was too complex, too expensive, and didn't work terribly well.

Nonetheless, through the efforts of Rolt, FFD refined and developed its four-wheel-drive technology, which included a viscous-coupling transfer unit. The FFD system had real benefits, but sadly these were never fully realised with the Capri. Dogged by technical issues and component failure (typically the CV joints, which were not of FFD manufacture) Ford quickly realised that the four-wheel-drive Capri project was going nowhere. As has already been pointed out, the Capri had never been designed as a four-wheel-drive car. Had it been, then the floorpan and the general layout of the underpinnings would have been designed to facilitate this.

The project was finally cancelled due to the pressure of the Escort rally programme and the sheer amount of work involved. Development of the four-wheel-drive Capri proved to be a steep learning curve for all involved, but there is no doubt that it helped pave the way for the four-wheel-drive Sierra of the early 1990s.

THE AMERICAN CONNECTION

Less well known, virtually overlooked even, is that a batch of four-wheel-drive Capris were sold in the USA. Inspired by the Capri's rallycross programme, in 1974 FF4 Automobiles of New York arranged to have 16 US-certified Capris shipped from Cologne to Ferguson Formula Developments near Coventry. All 16 had their front suspensions removed and a new subframe installed (this replaced the original cross-member). By reshaping the sump, FFD managed to find enough space for the aluminium-cased differential and half-shafts. All used the Ford C4 automatic transmission, the tailshaft of which was replaced by a centre differential complete with viscous coupling. The torque was split 37% front/63% rear. Interestingly, this was the 'new' viscous coupling and it was 15% smaller and 35% lighter than the one that the UK four-wheel-drive Capri had been saddled with.

Capris in rallying

Rallies would feature predominantly during the Capri's first few years. Having done so well in events such as the London to Sydney Marathon, and with the new Escort proving to be almost unbeatable, Ford of Europe reasoned that rallying, rather than racing, would bring them the success they coveted for the Capri. For the most part it did.

The Capri's first rally success occurred in March 1969 on the Internationale Rallye Lyon-Charbonnières. Driven by Dieter Glemser (who was partnered with Klaus Kaiser), the works Capri 2300GT finished a very fine fourth overall. On the same event Jean Francis Piot took his 2300GT to seventh overall (Jean Todt is often credited with being Piot's co-driver; in fact it was José Behra). The car was run in the Prototype Class. The Piot/Behra 2300GT then went on to win its class and finish sixth overall on the 1969 Tour de France. It also finished a superb third overall on the 1969 Tour de Corse.

Then, in 1970, things went slightly awry for the Capri in rallying. In particular it was the East African Safari Rally – a rally that held WRC (World Rally Championship) status until 2003 – which proved to be the Capri's undoing. Unfortunately, and although the 190bhp Capri 2300GTs had the pace (Rauno Aaltonen's Capri actually led the early stages), they couldn't take the punishment that the Safari dished out. Not one Capri finished the event.

Not that the Capri's rallying career was over. Far from it! Ford of France was hugely successful with its Group 2 specification Capri in European tarmac rallies with drivers such as Jean Vinatier and Guy Chausseuil, who scored numerous class wins. Vinatier took third overall and the class win on the 1972 Tour de France (behind two Ferrari Daytona 365GTs) in his BP-sponsored Capri, a car that Boreham had a hand in.

CAPRI RALLYING IN NORTH AMERICA

The Capri also had a successful rally career in North America. A number of Capris contested North American events over the years and some still do. Out of the 16 cars converted by Ferguson and sold by FF4 Automobiles in New York, one was converted to full rally specification. The stock 2.6-litre V6 was removed and replaced with a 200bhp, triple-downdraft, three-port, blueprinted Weslake V6. A full roll-cage was fitted, as were special-order 15in magnesium Minilites, and a host of other rally equipment. Owned by Doctor Loyal Jordar of Michigan, this car was rallied with moderate success in the US in the mid- to late 1970s. The SCCA Pro Rally Jordar/Ferguson Capri was the first four-wheel-drive car to be used in North American rallying. It currently resides in the Team Blitz stable of Capris.

Team Blitz won the 2007 Canadian Group 2 Forest Rally Championship, with driver Norm Murdock and navigator Larry Wells, in a 1971 two-wheel-drive Capri. A good number of Capris were

↓ **Team Blitz Rally Capri, winner of the 2007 Canadian Group 2 Forest Rally Championship. (Team Blitz)**

↑ **The Capri was one of the key players in the British Saloon Car Championship, especially in the mid- to late 1970s. (Ford Motor Company)**

used in NARRA and SCCA performance rallying back in the 1970s and 1980s, in events like the Sunriser 400 and Press On Regardless. Jeff Lantz won two Group 2 rally championships in Ontario, Canada, with his historic Capri.

Capri racing in Britain

Although Capris appeared on the race circuits soon after their original launch, the official racing Capri programme actually began on 15 March 1970, at Monza (their British debut was in September that year, at Silverstone).

Not that the Capri was greeted with open arms. Unsurprisingly, considering that the Capri was almost universally regarded as being a 2+2 and not a genuine four-seater, there was strong resistance against it being allowed to compete in the British Saloon Car Championship. Porsche's 911 had been outlawed at the end of the 1969 season for exactly the same reason.

Eventually, after it had been busy with its tape measures, the FIA announced that the Capri did, albeit marginally, meet the requisite cabin

dimensions. Nonetheless, the time taken to do this meant that the Capri didn't officially make it on to a British Saloon Car Championship grid until 1971 (which just happened to be around the time that the engine reliability problems had been overcome).

A number of racing Capris appeared, although it was Broadspeed who truly took up the Capri mantle and built two stunning RS2600s. One was for the UK; the other was headed for Belgium. As was the norm for Broadspeed, the cars were immaculately prepared, superbly built, and beautifully turned out, but they did push the boundaries of homologation. Ralph Broad, always eager to give the scrutineers a workout, designed a controversial suspension layout … amongst other things. The UK-based car was driven by the very talented Dave Matthews. Matthews, who finished second in the British Saloon Car Championship in 1972, found the Group 2 Capri to be more of a handful than the Escort, and the best he could manage was a third and a sixth overall. Tragically, a huge accident at Silverstone claimed the Capri (and would also later claim the life of a Mini driver who was involved in the accident).

↑ Gordon Spice was
one of Britain's top Capri
racers and ran a very
successful racing team.
These are two of the
team's 1978 racecars and
a roadgoing X-pack.
(Ford Motor Company)

← Stuart Graham had a
great run of success in the
Fabergé Brut 33 Capri.
(Ford Motor Company)

Pushing the performance envelope was the
name of the game. Or at least, it was when the
engines stayed in one piece! Brian Muir's Wiggins
Teape-sponsored Capri (a full works-specification
car, blessed with even more power than any
other contemporary race Capri) was capable of
mixing it with the big-engined American muscle
cars that were so much a part of the British racing
scene. Sadly, it wasn't capable of lasting the course
and suffered from numerous catastrophic and
embarrassing engine failures. (On many occasions
the reciprocating components within the Capri's
engine would make a successful bid for freedom.)
Ford actively chased publicity, but racetracks strewn
with the innards rent from various overworked Ford
V6 engines wasn't the type of exposure it coveted!
There were collective sighs of relief when Ford
managed to overcome these problems. From mid-
1971 the Capri not only had stunning pace, it had
reliability too – more on this anon.

CHANGING TIMES

You could legislate for many things in racing, but what you couldn't legislate for was the arrival of an energy crisis. The crisis of 1973 impacted heavily on motor sport and the Capri. What with Ford having to reduce its budget, and with the new Group 1 regulations imminent, the Capri racing programme was put on the back burner for a while.

Thankfully, the Capri soon had somewhere to showcase its talents. In 1973 the BRSCC organised the inaugural Tour of Britain, a multi-discipline event for Group 1 cars. Ford, and the Capri, were well represented. There were works Capris (with 160bhp) for Roger Clark, Dave Matthews, and Prince Michael of Kent, and a number of privately entered cars. A Capri didn't win the event (Clark led for quite some time before his Capri was sidelined by electrical gremlins), but Gordon Spice managed an excellent second place behind the event's surprise winner, F1 ace James Hunt, who'd done remarkably well to manhandle his 5.0-litre Chevrolet Camaro around what was a very demanding, varied, and challenging course.

The Tour of Britain was a great publicity vehicle for Ford, but what it really wanted was to get back into the British Saloon Car Championship. Behind the scenes there was much in the way of canvassing and campaigning, with the result that Capris soon began to migrate their way back into the BSCC. Indeed, one of the Tour of Britain Capris (tuned

to 175bhp) was fielded by Tom Walkinshaw in the 1974 Championship, where it scooped the class title. The new Capri II soon made its debut in the BSCC, although the front-running cars were still American. Most of these transatlantic terrors had an embarrassment of power. Some even had 7.4-litre engines under their lengthy, pulsating bonnets! Although unwieldy in the tighter corners, their straight-line pace was eye-watering.

Due to the transatlantic dominance of what was (and still is) our premier tin-top series, the RAC decided to play the patriotism card. It rejigged the rules for 1976, setting the new top limit at just 3.0 litres. Not that this played into the Capri's hands, as the championship still favoured the consistent class winner. Between 1975 and 1979 the championship fell to the Dolomite Sprint, Avenger, and Mini 1275GT. Even the Capri III, which had arrived in 1977 and would be developed to the point where it was producing a reliable 255bhp, couldn't take the championship, but it did amass plenty of race wins.

The late 1970s were effectively the high-water mark for the BSCC Capri. As the years went by the Capri began to fall out of favour, and would eventually become beached by regulations, old age, and corporate vacillation.

Ford wasn't really backing the Capri any more and its BSCC misery was compounded by the arrival, in 1980, of a new 3.5-litre class limit

↓ **Chris Craft racing his Hammonds Sauce Group 2 Capri II 3.0S at Silverstone in 1977. (Ford Motor Company)**

← Two historic racing Capris. (Gary Hawkins Photography)

↓ Replica Texaco Group I Capri. (Gary Hawkins Photography)

which allowed V8 Rovers to compete. This was a somewhat contentious move as the Rovers were actually 3,528cc, but with some subtle and judicious manipulation of the rules they snuck in. Not that the Rovers found the championship to be a walkover. Far from it. The brilliant Andy Rouse did win the championship in 1984, driving a Rover Vitesse, but for three years prior to this it was Win Percy who triumphed. Percy won in 1980 in his RX7, did the RX7 double in 1981, and then scored the hat-trick in 1982 with a Toyota Corolla. The Capris dominated many of the races, but it was Percy's class dominance that won through for Toyota and Mazda.

What actually signalled the end of the road for the Capri in British racing was the arrival of Group A in 1983. The soon to be dominant Merkur/Sierra was about to be unleashed and, realising that the Capri 2.8i would require a lot of development

if it was to be competitive, Ford threw its weight behind the Sierra. The feeling that emanated from within Ford was that the Capri, a former design leader and race winner, was now rather passé. Even if it had continued to support the Capri, Ford reasoned that the 2.8 injection engine was not an ideal competition unit and would require a lot of work to make it one. This was not actually true. Ford had amassed a huge amount of Cologne engine experience and it wouldn't have been impossible to extract a serious amount of power from the 2.8. Nevertheless, Ford didn't want to proceed, and the upshot of this sea change in Capri fortunes was that only four Capris took part during the 1983 season. In fact this season proved to be a rather unsatisfactory and strife-ridden affair thanks to the questionable eligibility of the works Rovers.

The Capri's British Saloon Car Championship career may have been over, but it would continue

↑ **Fast but flawed. The racing RS2600s had style, pace, but not the downforce. Despite this they were developed into hugely successful, race-winning cars, largely thanks to the skill of the competition department's personnel and the calibre of the drivers that Ford employed. (Ford Motor Company)**

to be part of the UK racing scene. GAA V6, V8, and even DFV-powered Capris were dominant in the Thundersaloon series amongst others. The Capri has also experienced a relatively recent and considerable resurgence in interest thanks to the strength of the UK's various classic/historic race series.

Capri racing in Europe

Over in Cologne, as the 1970s unfolded, Kranefuss and Braungart had come to the realisation that the Capri's sporting future lay in racing and not rallying. They were acutely aware of what could be achieved if the company sanctioned the building of a special series Capri, a homologation special in fact. What was needed was a Capri that would fit within the over 2.5-litres class and could be taken to 3.0 litres and possibly beyond. With great support from Walter Hayes, other Ford luminaries, and Boreham, the car that would become the Capri RS2600 began to take shape. In the meantime, it was left to the other Capri models to pick up the racing baton and run with it.

Painted silver and blue, fitted with split-rim wheels, pop-riveted arch extensions, the beginnings of a front spoiler, and based on the 2300GT, the racing Capris certainly looked the part. They performed well too. Unfortunately they could

not perform well enough for long enough! The Weslake-modified 2300GT engines, with special aluminium heads and a raft of other upgrades, were plagued with reliability issues.

Dismayed by the 2300GT's woeful reliability record and subsequent lack of finishes, Neerpasch was on the verge of resigning. Fortuitously, in November 1970 Peter Ashcroft – Ford's competition manager, and an ace engine builder – was seconded to Cologne for a period of six months.

Having investigated the remnants of the various racing V6 engines that hadn't lasted the course, and following an in-depth analysis of the V6's workings (and a number of protracted conversations with Keith Duckworth at Cosworth), Ashcroft set about reinventing the Cologne V6. He drew up a list of must-have components, which included steel rods, a dry-sump system (until his arrival they were still running wet sumps), and a new design of steel crank. The existing crankshaft was completely the wrong design – due to its out of balance harmonics it was literally shaking the engine to pieces – so Ashcroft got Weslake to manufacture a new design of steel crank and a set of stronger main bearing caps. He also sanctioned the production of a much more rigid engine block, which would eventually find its way into production cars such as the Federal 2800.

Although the 2300GT was now performing beautifully, its tenure at the top was coming to an end. In October 1970 Ford had displayed a prototype RS2600 at Geneva, by which time it had managed to manoeuvre the RS2600 programme through the homologation process.

Ashcroft's involvement in the development of the RS2600 should not be overlooked. He not only managed to sort out the engine reliability problems and find ways of increasing the capacity to almost 3.0 litres, he also played a big part in getting the production RS2600 sorted. What's more, he undoubtedly played a huge part in bringing Boreham and Cologne much closer together, although the German cars were always known by their generic name, ie the Cologne Capri.

Not only did the engine prove to be more reliable (it couldn't have been less reliable!), with its lightened flywheel, bigger valves, different cam profile, higher-compression pistons, and re-calibrated injection, the power was a heady 260bhp. Prior to this the best that had been seen from the engine was 220bhp. Over a short period of time the capacity grew, and so too did the power. The best 2,940cc engines were soon generating 285bhp and staying together for the length of an endurance race, where the Capris were almost touching 160mph. By 1973 the power had risen to 325bhp.

Braungart had also brought a wealth of experience to Ford, and he revolutionised the way the competition department tackled its racing. The Capri 2300GTs had been well-modified road cars, but the RS2600 racecars only paid lip service to their road car roots. Every modification was approved and the racers sported fabricated suspension parts, bespoke damping, proper axle location, formula car braking systems, beautifully blended-in arches, lowered and repositioned engines, and careful weight distribution to reduce the car's nose-heavy bias. Racing is a boundary-pushing exercise and the Capri's leaf-spring rear suspension was particularly creative. To comply with the rules, a thin leaf-spring was retained, but it was the 'helper' coil springs that did all of the work.

Not that the handling was without its issues. In extremis the Capri RS2600 would lift one, two, and sometimes three wheels off the ground, and even the most talented and fearless of drivers

↓ 1973: Ford v BMW – the wings win through, but the Capris slugged it out until the end of the season, with some excellent results. (Ford Motor Company)

could be reduced to nervous wrecks. Even the mega-talented Jackie Stewart was not a fan of the RS2600, but he was contractually obliged to drive it when requested. That said, Dieter Glemser, Jochen Mass, and Hans Heyer were not intimidated by the Capri RS2600 and would regularly out-run the F1 aces.

The driver line-up for the 1971 season included John Fitzpatrick, Jerry Birrell, Dieter Glemser, Dr Helmut Marko, Francois Mazet, and Alex Soler-Roig, with one-off appearances planned for Kurt Ahrens, Jean Pierre Jabouille, Graham Hill, and John Surtees.

It would be nice to report that the RS2600s had a fairy-tale debut in the 1971 European Touring Car Championship, but they didn't. Glemser/Soler-Roig led, but the head gasket let go. Following valve spring woes Marko's Capri was eventually classified tenth. However, from round 2, with gasket sealing rings fitted into grooves machined into the cylinder block, everything went exactly as Ford hoped it would, and it was soon a case of follow the (Capri) leader.

During the 1971 and 1972 seasons the RS2600s were only ever beaten on three occasions, and one of these was by an Escort. The engines would eventually peak at 325bhp and reliability was generally excellent. In two seasons, the RS2600 won 13 out of 16 races in the European Touring Car Championship,

Jochen Mass took the win in the German National Championship (Rundstreckenmeisterschaft), and Dieter Glemser secured the 1971 Driver's title at the series' dramatic finale at Jarama.

Also dramatic was the unexpected departure (just after the 1972 season had started) of Jochen Neerpasch and Martin Braungart, who defected to arch-rival BMW. There were sound reasons for their move; it was just that it was unexpected and unfortunate. Fortunately, Mike Kranefuss stepped up the mark and did a fantastic job. He was joined by former NSU racer and development engineer Thomas Ammerschlager, who took over where Martin Braungart had left off.

Development of the 1972 season RS2600s had focused on improving the suspension (a much more sophisticated coil-sprung rear end was fitted and the McPherson struts were equipped with a multi-hole top mount for adjustability) and the structural integrity, by using the roll-cage as a part of the car's structure. One of the biggest improvements came as a result of switching from 13in to 15in wheels, which allowed for the fitment of bigger brakes and better tyres. A number of the drivetrain components were lightened, although the cars still tipped the scales at around 980kg, some 80kg over the homologated minimum weight, which was akin to carrying a passenger!

Still, in 1972 the Cologne Capris triumphed in eight out of nine races, beating the likes of the Chevrolet Camaro, AMG Mercedes, Opel Commodore Alpina BMW, Broadspeed Escort, and Alfa Romeo. At the Spa 24-hour race the Capris finished 1-2-3, with Jochen Mass and fellow ex-Formula 1 driver Hans Stuck winning, Gerry Birrell together with Claude Bourgoignie finishing second, and Glemser and Soler-Roig finishing third.

There was much racing Capri toing and froing, of course. UK cars would regularly race overseas, and vice versa. This resulted in many great battles, and one in particular stands out.

Sharing the car with John Miles, Brian Muir won the six-hour race at Paul Ricard in the Malcolm Gartlan Racing Capri RS2600. Jackie Stewart and Francois Cevert were in one Ford Cologne Capri; Gérard Larrousse, Alex Soler-Roig, and Jochen Mass were sharing another. The Miles/Muir car was exceptionally quick and less thirsty too, thanks to its 1973 specification and fuel-efficient Weslake engine. This was exactly the type of engine that Weslake had been trying to persuade the factory to run (but the factory doggedly stuck with the 1972-specification engines). The Miles/Muir victory caused huge embarrassment to Ford of Germany and its Cologne competition department, and left a sour taste for years to come. Ford had fully expected to win, but the Cologne cars couldn't quite match the pace of the Miles/Muir car. Not that this was perceived to be a problem, as Ford expected to snatch the lead from Miles/Muir when it came in for its third petrol stop. Except it didn't need that petrol stop because the engine modifications had also made it less thirsty. Thanks to engineering skill, and pure driving ability, Miles/Muir won through. It was a truly magnificent victory, however, and well deserved. As the old adage goes, 'to finish first, you must first finish'. The works Capris had barely time to cool down before Kranefuss was overseeing the installation of 1973-specification engines in the works Capris!

The RS2600s had really shone in what was an increasingly competitive championship. Nevertheless, the competition was upping its game. If Ford was to win in 1973 it, too, needed to up its game and spend more money … a lot more money. BMW intended fielding a fleet of its recently homologated, lightweight CSL coupes, and its assault on the championship would cost the company well over £1 million. However, rather than match BMW financially Ford provided

Kranefuss with the same budget as he'd had for 1972. With the upgrades needed, and the extra investment in materials and manpower, not to mention salaries, this simply wasn't enough. And if this wasn't bad enough, BMW also had a support network of semi-works teams such as Schnitzer and Alpina, who'd also be running CSLs.

To try and close the gap, Ford had managed to homologate a new aero package: even wider 16in wheels, under-bonnet improvements, and 325bhp engines. By 1972's standards the RS2600 was a great car – but this was 1973. Kranefuss tried to get a rear wing homologated, to no avail. The rear wing was essential, as drivers were reporting that the rears of their Capris were lifting at speed. Even the sublimely talented Jackie Stewart found the RS2600 to be a real handful to drive. So too did Emerson Fittipaldi. In the end it was the lack of a Capri rear wing and the arrival of a BMW wing that pushed things in BMW's favour.

Thanks to the eagle-eyed Neerpasch and Braungart, who spotted an FIA amendment (loophole?) which apparently allowed BMW to fit wings to their coupes (race and road), BMW swung into action and within a space of just six weeks the BMW coupe had grown wings. Due to its striking appearance, the car was immediately dubbed the 'Batmobile'. These staggeringly successful aerodynamic appendages slashed lap times, times that were further reduced with the arrival of the new 3.5-litre engine in July. Ford would pay dearly for its tardiness and for not listening to what Neerpasch had told them regarding the must-have wing. Ford's drivers did their utmost to wring every ounce of performance from the wingless Capris, putting themselves at great risk in the process. To show just how effective the BMW's aero pack was, at the 1973 Silverstone TT the second-placed Capri was three laps adrift. Or to put it another way, almost nine miles behind!

Not that this was Ford or Kranefuss's fault. They had been assured that BMW would not be able to homologate the aero package in time. But unfortunately, and rather unsportingly, Neerpasch had somehow managed to include an update in the FIA papers. This was done in the spring of 1973. It was largely down to the fact that the FIA accepted the update, and Kranefuss had not contested it, that the 1973

↑ **The iconic and seriously potent quad-cam, 32-valve, Ford-Cosworth GAA-V6. (Ford Motor Company)**

season would swing in BMW's favour. It was still an exceptionally close battle, however, and the Capris pushed the BMWs very hard indeed. In fact, in the DRM Hans Heyer triumphed over the BMWs in his works 2.9-litre Capri.

THE RS3100

The Weslake V6 had been developed to the point where it was producing very good power, and with reliability. Unfortunately, and despite the company's best efforts, more power was needed, as were more engines. Weslake just didn't have the capacity for producing a continuous run of larger capacity and more powerful long-distance racing engines. But Cosworth did.

During 1973 Ford switched allegiance to acknowledged engine experts Cosworth Engineering. Work had already begun on producing a new production-based engine for the 1974 season (something that Jochen Neerpasch, who had defected to BMW, was completely unaware of). In fact Neerpasch actually approached Cosworth and asked for assistance with the BMW straight-six engine.

Naturally, due to their commitment with Ford they were unable to help him.

During discussions with Cosworth, Ford decided that it was feasible to produce a 3.1-litre engine that could be installed in a small run of roadgoing Capris. Then, by using the standard roadgoing Essex V6 block and the standard stroke (72.42mm), but a monster 100mm bore size and special Cosworth forged pistons, the capacity would balloon to 3,412cc.

Although based on the production block, everything else about the engine would be bespoke. The Cosworth GAA, as it would become known, featured special aluminium cylinder heads, belt-driven double-overhead camshafts on each bank of cylinders, 24 valves, Luca fuel injection, Lucas Rita transistorised ignition, and dry-sumping. Problems with the bottom end led to delays whilst a legal and strength-inducing solution was found. Once this had been sorted, the GAA was trialled on the dyno, where it ran reliably and breezed past the 415bhp mark. As the season progressed and the engine was developed, it would soon be producing a reliable 455bhp – enough to give the Capri a top speed of around 186mph.

To put this into context, on its introduction the all-conquering Ford-Cosworth DFV Formula 1 engine delivered 408bhp at 9,000rpm. By 1983, the last year the DFV won an F1 race, the power had only risen to 500bhp.

With this amount of power on tap, the RS3100 needed proper aerodynamics and a great chassis. Fortunately the racing RS3100 was blessed with both.

The real handling improvement was provided by the new aerodynamic package. The front downforce could be trimmed via slats in the front spoiler, but the big news was the 'ducktail' rear spoiler. This much-needed item really pinned the back of the Capri to the ground.

In terms of its chassis, the RS3100 was actually very similar to the RS2600. The 'infamous' plastic leaf-springs remained and the rest of the rear suspension system was composed of alloy-cased Bilstein coilovers, radius arms, anti-roll bar, Watt's linkage, and Atlas axle. To improve the roll stiffness, the spring rates would increase as the season unfolded and the rear springs would be moved out as far towards the sides of the car as was physically possible. The front suspension was as before, although it was now equipped with magnesium hub carriers (also used at the rear). Magnesium was not just strong; it had the advantage of being light for a given size. This was important, as weight was always an issue. Due to having to run with a lot more in the way of metal panelling than the RS2600, and the heavier engine etc, the RS3100 weighed in at around 1,050kg. It was a heavy car, which required seriously effective brakes.

And it got some. Because the wheels were now 16in in diameter (16in wheels had been trialled for most of the 1973 season), it was possible to fit much larger brakes than before. Up front there were 11.9in ventilated discs, while the rears were 11.5in. These dustbin-lid-sized discs certainly helped, but the real improvement came from a special electro-hydraulic pumping system, which reacted with great speed and sensitivity. The real trick, however, was the hidden water-cooling system. The engineers had installed a washer reservoir well away from the scrutineers' prying eyes … it was inside the passenger seat! The water was pumped to all four wheels by means of a screen washer. Carefully positioned jets would then squirt water into the vents of the discs. Understandably, the temperature of the disc plummeted, the water evaporated, and fade-free braking was virtually guaranteed.

Engine cooling was another issue that the team had to overcome. Having experimented with a rear-mounted radiator that didn't really work, two radiators were mounted in the side wings and the front air intake was blanked off.

To reduce the car's noseweight, many of the car's auxiliaries (oil cooler, diff cooler, fuel tank, etc) had been mounted as low and as far back as possible. Transmission was a ZF five-speeder, which drove through a triple-plate clutch.

Inevitably there were some reliability and teething issues, but the Capris soon outpaced the BMWs (which by now had been equipped with 24-valve, 3.5-litre engines). During 1974 and 1975 the Capris contested 17 races, won eight times, finished second six times, and third once. BMW didn't have such a good time, especially at the 1974 Nürburgring, where the attrition rate proved to be very high. High enough, in fact, for BMW to pull out

↓ Racing RS2600s were fast, but far from easy to drive. (Paul Kooyman)

← Bravery required – especially in the wet! (Paul Kooyman)

of the championship, leaving it to the semi-works and privateer BMWs to fight it out with the Capris.

Neither Ford nor BMW took any official interest in the 1975 championship. Nonetheless, a number of RS3100s were raced, successfully too, but in the hands of privateers. The year 1975 proved to be a far from vintage one for Ford. AVO was closed (the competition department at Cologne had shut down the year before), and the last appearance by a factory Cologne Capri RS3100 was at Kyalami on 1 November. Driven by Mass/Ludwig, it retired due to engine failure.

The RS3100 never really got the support and financial backing it needed and deserved. Despite this, the teams behind it were amongst the best in the world, and it was their commitment, drive, and sheer hard work that put the RS3100 in front.

The RS3100 is a touring car giant and it truly deserves the accolades that are heaped upon it.

THE ZAKSPEED GROUP 5 CAPRIS

In the 1970s the name Zakspeed was synonymous with some of the best-prepared, best-looking, and quickest Escorts around, and they soon became the scourge of Europe. Zakspeed was the brainchild of Former East German refugee Erich Zakowski. Having started up his business with one small garage, he later progressed to a Ford car and truck franchise. The tuning and preparation side of the business expanded in a similar fashion, and by the 1970s Zakspeed was a motorsports phenomenon. Although the Escorts established the company's reputation as a front-runner and master tuner, it was its mastery with the later Capris that cemented this reputation.

Touring car racing in Germany was huge in the 1970s; 1972 saw the introduction of a new national series, the Deutsche Rennsport Meisterschaft (DRM). Having persevered with the FIA Group 2 and Group 4 rules, the series switched to Group 5 in 1977, which proved to be very successful ... for a while. Division 1 catered for cars with engine capacities from 2,000cc to 2,500cc, Division 2 for those under 2,000cc. Zakspeed was the official Ford team in the DRM.

A rash of lean and lithe turbocharged cars began to appear. By comparison, the Zakspeed Escorts were rather breathless. So a plan was hatched. To reassert Zakspeed's rightful position, at the front, Eric Zakowski and his team made the

↑ → **Modelling and testing the scale-model Group 5 Zakspeed Capris. (Ford Motor Company)**

switch to forced induction. And it was around this tine that Ford showed its corporate hand. Keen to engender more interest in the Capri, and with no in-house specialist department to call upon, it turned to Zakspeed to construct, develop, and race a rather special breed of Capri III – the Zakspeed Group 5 Capri, which was unveiled and first raced at Hockenheim in September 1978. Driven by Hans Heyer, it led before engine trouble forced it to a halt. Heyer would use this Mampe-sponsored car to good effect later in the season, taking three poles and winning at the Nürburgring. Heyer would be joined by racing journalist Harald Ertl, who had moved over from BMW. (Ertl was one of the four F1 drivers who pulled Nicki Lauda from the wreck of his flaming Ferrari at the Nürburgring in 1976. Lauda suffered severe facial burns and other injuries, but was saved by the actions of Ertl, Guy Edwards, Brett Lunger, and Arturo Merzario.)

There is no doubt that the racing versions of the RS2600 and certainly the RS3100 stretched the umbilical link with the road versions to the very limit. Racing pushes boundaries, pushes technology, and pushes teams to investigate the rulebook in their quest for loopholes and technical twists. The racing RS Capris were feral, often nihilistic creations, but in comparison with the Zakspeed Capris they appear almost tame. Introduced for Group 5 racing in Germany, and ostensibly based on the recently launched Capri III, the Zakspeed Turbo Capris were slimmed-down and savagely powerful incarnations that had only the merest link with their showroom counterparts.

↑ The Zakspeed Team. (Ford Motor Company)

Owing much to the lightweight and technically advanced Zakspeed Escorts, the Zakspeed Capris evolved in much the same way as the Super Saloon cars did in the UK. There was the merest hint, the smallest soupçon, of the production car in the Zakspeed Capri's construction: it retained the standard car's windscreen surround, side-window surrounds, rear-window surround, and enough of the upper rear body to maintain its characteristic body style.

The Zakspeed Capri had looks to die for, and they were recognisable as Capris. But they had real beauty, a beauty that was more than skin deep … much more.

Roll-cage technology had come on in leaps and bounds and Zakspeed was at the forefront of the

↑ ↑ National pride: the Group 5 Zakspeed Capris featured German technology and sponsorship. This is Klaus Ludwig in the 1981 championship-winning Division 2 'Würth' Capri. (Ford Motor Company)

latest technology. The Zakspeed Capris were, in effect, lightly clothed roll-cages with an engine. The roll-cage, a skeletal and space-framed device, was constructed out of aluminium tubing that varied in diameter depending on the loading and structural requirements. The air jacks were also incorporated into the structure at this stage. As for the bodywork, that was crafted from Kevlar 49 and featured detachable front and rear wings, detachable bonnet and front spoiler. Initially the rear wing was moulded into the rear body section.

The engine chosen for the assault on the DRM series was a turbocharged version of the race- and rally-winning four-cylinder Ford Cosworth BDA, which was based on the Kent 1300 production block. Early engines, which produced 380bhp at 9,000rpm, were built by Zakspeed using Cosworth components in their entirety. The actual capacity was 1,427cc. When the internationally agreed forced induction multiplication factor of 1.4 was applied, this equated to 1,997.8cc, thus bringing it in just under the 2,000cc Division 2 ceiling. Later engines were also built by Zakspeed but only after consultation with Schrick, a German company that has long been at the forefront of component manufacture and supply to the motorsports industry. The engines were fitted with parts supplied by various specialist German companies, Schrick included.

This was not done to snub Cosworth; it was just that German companies have a long tradition of developing their own cars and they have always done so in conjunction with other national companies.

The engines were soon delivering a reliable 460bhp. Reliable is good, but when Ford realised that – despite the considerable power output – the Capri would always be at a power disadvantage compared to the all-conquering Porsche 935, it sanctioned the building of a bigger, Division 1 engine. Zakspeed got creative!

Using a turbocharged 1500 engine, in September 1979 Hans Heyer took his Division 1 Capri to third place overall at Hockenheim. Encouraged, Zakspeed's boffins began work on a 'proper' Division 1 Capri. The engine, whilst still based on the Kent-blocked BDA, had its capacity up to 1,745cc, which, with the 1.4 multiplication factor, boosted it to 2,443cc, comfortably inside Division 1's 2,500cc limit. Power output was a staggering 560bhp (which translates into an incredible 312bhp/ litre). In a car that tipped the scales at just 790kg the performance was electrifying.

Division 2 cars could touch 174mph, with the Division 1 cars being capable of 186mph. Sources have suggested that as the 1980 season progressed, the 1,745cc engines actually produced over 600bhp and the 1,427cc versions were giving in excess of 500bhp. A twin turbo installation was trialled on the 1,745cc engine, but as it wasn't found to give any significant advantage the team reverted to the single.

Klaus Ludwig had joined the team to drive in Division 1 and a run of success followed. However, Zakspeed had done some work to the rear wing, making it larger, and its width was slightly greater than before and consequently sat slightly wide of the rear wheelarches. This new design was eventually outlawed and Ludwig was stripped of the points he had scored at Zolder and the Nürburgring. Zakspeed's response to this was that from the summer of 1980 on, the cars ran with a central 'ground effect' tunnel and fixed side skirts. Ludwig went on to win Division 1, although the points deducted relegated him to third overall in the championship. In 1981 Ludwig switched to Division 2 and with 11 wins in this category he took the win and the DRM title.

Ford, and Zakspeed, had a tremendous run of success with the Group 5 Capris, winning the DRM championship in 1981. The move to Group C didn't do the Capri any favours and the cars (which were raced until 1983) slipped down the order. Nevertheless, the Zakspeed Capris had more than their fair share of glory, and shall go down in the annals of motor-racing history as being amongst the most successful, and certainly the most extreme, Capris ever.

To incorporate the new Group C and Group 6 sports prototype cars, the two-division structure was abandoned in 1982. Zakspeed and Ford used the season to develop the Ford C100 but also raced a Division 1 Capri in several rounds. Ludwig switched between the two cars (both were in a new bright orange Jagermeister livery), while Klaus Neidzwiedz raced a stripe-liveried D&W car.

Zakspeed was also commissioned by Ford USA's Special Vehicle Operations to produce a 1,745cc Mustang, which competed in the IMSA GT series.

The RS3100 returns

The Bourgoignie Broadspeed/Cologne RS3100 was returned to the UK in 1973 and was driven by Andy Rouse at the Tourist Trophy meeting and then sold to Bo Emanuelson, who won the Swedish championship in 1974. In 1975 it was returned to Ford Cologne, where it was rebuilt to the latest specification including Ford Cosworth GAA-V6 engine. Bo won many races in Sweden and Europe, being faster than Jochen Mass at the Nürburgring. When Sweden imposed a 2-litre limit in 1976 the car, being 3.4 litres, became obsolete. It was purchased by Vince Woodman and successfully campaigned in Thundersaloon races in the UK. After 22 years in dry storage a complete restoration was undertaken by QM engineering in March 2006, which involved stripping to the bare shell, sand blasting and reinforcing the roll-cage, then resealing the body painting and exterior in preparation for a total restoration, which included full engine rebuild by Swindon Racing Engines.

The rebuild took 14 months, but this charismatic and iconic car is now racing and winning once again.

Vince Woodman's stunning Broadspeed/ Cologne RS3100. (Chris Brown)

Although ostensibly a Mustang Mach 1, in reality it was a reskinned Group 5 Capri. The director of SVO was none other than Mike Kranefuss. He rebuilt Ford's long-dormant North American racing programme, and the car which started that programme was the Zakspeed Capri/Mustang. The Capri/Mustang link had come full circle.

Capri racing in America

The Capri was also raced successfully in the USA. The team of Horst Kwech and Harry Theodoracopulos competed in Trans Am and IMSA GT racing during the mid-1970s with both Weslake and GAA motivated cars. One of these was the ex-Muir car from Spa, which was destroyed in a shunt at Watkins Glen and had to be re-shelled using a NA-spec standard shell. Kwech went on to partner with Lee Dykstra in the making of the Dekon Monza IMSA GT car for Chevrolet.

And there was some success with stock Capris running in SCCA showroom stock road-racing during the late 1970s. Interestingly, several Capris were used for short track dirt and pavement oval racing, usually with American V8 powerplants. There was even a Baby Grand National Capri II raced by Dale Jarrett in NASCAR (years before he eventually won the Winston Cup season championship in the top-level division). In more recent times Team Blitz's 2.0-litre Pinto-powered Capri won the SCCA's top-contested Central Division in 1986 and 1987, taking over 90% of the wins along the way.

Capri racing in South Africa

Driving one of the Team Gunston Capri Perana V8s (race number Z181), Bob Olthoff won the 1970 South African Saloon Car Championship. Indeed, the car was too successful for its own good, as were a number of the Group 5 cars, resulting in a racing ban and new regulations being drawn up. Built to FIA Group 5 regulations, the Perana is supposed to have lapped Kyalami only eight seconds slower than a contemporary Formula 1 car. Peter Lindenburg found this forgotten Capri in 1987 and completely rebuilt it. It has been checked over by Basil Green. Peter races this charismatic car in historic events, where it still manages podium places.

In the UK, Richard Austin races a Perana replica in historic events. Built along the lines of the Team Gunston car, it uses a 351 V8 engine and is based on a left-hand-drive Mercury Capri

→ Team Blitz's ultra-
successful 2-litre Pinto-
powered Capri.
(Team Blitz)

→ Capri Perana
Racer. (Gary Hawkins
Photography)

that has been converted to right-hand drive. This car is exceptionally quick and very successful.

Capris on ice

The Capri was a very versatile car, versatile enough to be successful in ice racing. Timo Makinen used a Boreham Capri RS2600 to great effect in the 1972 Finnish Ice Racing Championship … he won it!

Technical specifications

2300GT – GROUP 2 RACING 1970
- **Engine** – 2.3-litre Weslake-modified Cologne V6 enlarged to 2,397cc, aluminium heads, Kugelfischer mechanical fuel injection. Power: 230bhp at 7,500rpm.
- **Gearbox** – Four-speed manual/ optional Borg-Warner Type 35 automatic, final drive 3.22:1.
- **Bodyshell** – Flared arches, alloy spoilers at front, then larger spoilers, pop-riveted arch extensions, roll-cage.
- **Wheels** – BBS aluminium or magnesium split-rims (8–10in front, 10in rear).
- **Tyres** – Dunlop in various patterns/ compounds.
- **Weight** – 940kg.
- **Maximum speed** – 143mph.

RS2600 – GROUP 2 RACING 1971
- **Engine** – 2.6-litre Weslake-modified Cologne V6 enlarged to 2,873cc, Kugelfischer mechanical fuel injection. Power: 275bhp at 7,300rpm.
- **Gearbox** – ZF five-speed.
- **Bodyshell** – GRP front and rear wings with arch extensions, riveted into bodyshell, GRP bonnet, boot, and doors, full-width front spoiler, improved roll-cage.
- **Wheels** – BBS split-rims (10 x 13in fronts, 11.5 x 13in rears).
- **Tyres** – Dunlop in various patterns/ compounds.
- **Weight** – 940kg.
- **Maximum speed** – 158mph.

RS2600 – GROUP 2 RACING 1972, 1973
- **Engine** – 2.6-litre Weslake-modified Cologne V6 enlarged to 2,995cc, Kugelfischer mechanical fuel injection. Power: 290bhp at 7,500rpm (1972), 325bhp at 7,600rpm (1973).
- **Gearbox** – ZF five-speed.
- **Bodyshell** – GRP front and rear wings with arch extensions, riveted into bodyshell, GRP bonnet, boot, and doors, wrap-around front spoiler, improved and fully integrated roll-cage.
- **Wheels** – BBS split-rims, 10–11 x 15in front, 12–14 x 15in rear (1972), 10–11 x 16in front, 12–14 x 16in rear (used for most of 1973 for experimentation).
- **Tyres** – Dunlop in various patterns/ compounds.
- **Weight** – 980kg.
- **Maximum speed** – 170mph.

RS3100 – GROUP 2 RACING
- **Engine** – 3.4-litre Essex V6, produced by Cosworth, 3412cc, Lucas injection (Kugelfischer injection on later cars). Power 415–455bhp@8,500rpm.
- **Gearbox** – Four-speed manual / optional limited slip differential, final drive 3.09:1.
- **Bodyshell** – Flared arches, roll-cage.
- **Wheels** – 12½in front, 15½in rear.
- **Tyres** – Dunlop in various patterns/ compounds.
- **Weight** – 1,040kg.
- **Maximum speed** – 186mph

ZAKSPEED CAPRI DIVISION 1 – GROUP 5 RACING
- **Engine** – Ford-Cosworth BDA, four-cylinder, 1,745cc, 560bhp at 9,000rpm.
- **Gearbox** – Four-speed manual (early 2.8 Injection gearbox), standard limited slip differential, final drive 3.09:1.
- **Bodyshell** – Spaceframe chassis with alloy roll-cage and Kevlar panelling.
- **Wheels** – 11in x 16in front, 14 x 19in rear.
- **Tyres** – Dunlop in various patterns/ compounds.
- **Weight** – 790kg.
- **Maximum speed** – 186mph.

ZAKSPEED CAPRI DIVISION 2 SPECIFICATION – GROUP 5 RACING
- **Engine** – Ford-Cosworth BDA, four-cylinder, 1,427cc, 460bhp at 9,000rpm.
- **Gearbox** – Four-speed manual (early 2.8 Injection gearbox), standard limited slip differential, final drive 3.09:1.
- **Bodyshell** – Spaceframe chassis with alloy roll-cage and Kevlar panelling.
- **Wheels** – 10 x 16in front, 12 x 19in rear.
- **Tyres** – Goodyear in various patterns/compounds.
- **Weight** – 790kg.
- **Maximum speed** – 174mph.

CHAPTER 7
CAPRI TUNERS AND MODIFIERS

Historically, ever since Ford became involved in motor sport it has produced cars that became the mainstay of the UK's proactive and pioneering tuning industry. Naturally, when the Capri arrived on the scene the tuners turned their attention to Ford's latest progeny almost en masse.

Although there was something of a rush to develop the Capri in its early years, the various tuners would continue to work their magic on it right up until production ended. Some are still involved with the Capri to this day.

Allard

The Allard Motor Company has always been heavily involved in motorsport since being founded by Sydney Allard in 1946. Sydney manufactured several cars, all of which were modified and built by him. Alan Allard was involved in dragsters and

rallying in the 1960s and 1970s, mixing with the likes of Roger Clark. The company also produced recognised Ford Anglia competition cars known as 'Allardettes', which were homologated Anglias with 997, 1,200 and 1,340cc supercharged engines. Sydney and Alan used these cars in several Monte Carlo and Spa–Sofia–Liège rallies, domestic rallies, and sprints.

Alan Allard was a forced induction pioneer, and in 1972 he introduced a supercharged Capri 3.0-litre. The conversion used specially modified cylinder heads, special Weslake gaskets, a free-flow exhaust system, an Allard-Wade supercharger, uprated suspension, a front spoiler, and a GRP 'blister' for the bonnet (to provide clearance for the supercharger). The cost of the conversion was £415 and the company offered new cars with the conversion for £1,978. Allard rev-limited the engine, which provided a top speed of 130mph and a 0–60mph time of just 6.8 seconds.

← **The mighty 5.7-litre V8 in the replica Perana Capri racer. (Gary Hawkins Photography)**

← **Supercharger kit. (Alan Allard)**

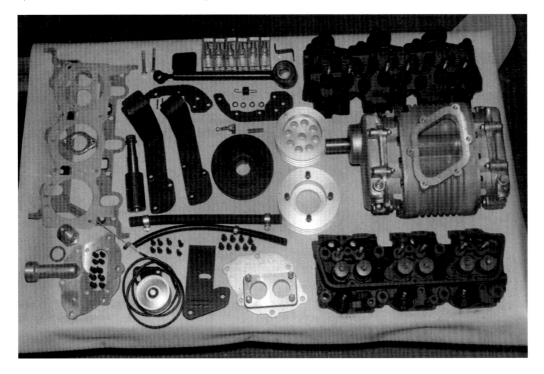

↑ Turbo installation on Broadspeed Bullit. (Gary Hawkins Photography)

↑ ↑ Broadspeed duo. (Gary Hawkins Photography)

system, Allard ensured that extra fuel was delivered when the engine was under load. Due to the clever engineering involved in the conversion, 95 octane fuel could still be used. Power was boosted (6.5psi maximum) from 160 to 210bhp. Top speed was in the region of 130mph due to the engine rpm being limited. Cost in 1984 was £1,295 plus VAT.

The company also produced a V8 version. Fitted with a 302 V8 giving 225bhp, the Allard V8 Capri went rather well but, due to the extra weight, proved to be a bit of a beast to drive. Cars were built to individual order.

Now trading as Allard Turbosport, the company continues to market and undertake similar high-quality conversions for a wide variety of cars (petrol and diesel) and is still heavily involved with motorsport and product development.

Broadspeed

The respected and legendary UK tuner Broadspeed was one of the most important and influential companies of its type during the 1960s and 1970s. It built some of the fastest Mini Cooper S racecars of the era, which more often than not were seen beating the works entries. In 1966 Broadspeed switched allegiance to Ford. The Broadspeed Anglias, Escorts, and Capris were always quick, successful, and immaculately prepared. Broadspeed

Having made its name through its work with supercharging, the company went on to produce a number of turbocharged conversions for a wide variety of cars, including the Capri.

As with its conversions on earlier Capris, Allard's Ford Capri 2.8i was a very professional engine upgrade that utilised an IHI RHB6 turbocharger (with integral wastegate), bespoke 17-row air-to-air intercooler, a large 16-row thermostatically controlled oil cooler, colder plugs, silicone plug leads, bespoke exhaust manifold, link pipe, and turbo discharge pipe. The compression ratio was reduced from 9.2:1 to 8.5:1 and the ignition curve was altered. The original exhaust system was retained. By modifying the injection was amongst the first to tackle the Capri from a performance angle.

Although Broadspeed would convert most Capri variants, especially the 1600GT, it was best known for its turbocharged terror, the Broadspeed Bullit. Available with a range of modifications and options, the famed Bullit 3.0-litre conversions were exceptionally well engineered. Turbocharging was in its infancy but Broadspeed nailed the process and delivered cars that were potent yet easy to drive and easy to live with. Customers could expect at least 175bhp for their investment, more if required.

April 1971's edition of *Motor Sport* carried a 'Performance Road Test' of the Bullit. The car found favour: 'The straight-line performance of the Bullit is impressive. The acceleration up to the UK speed limit being as good as, or slightly better than the 4.2-litre E-Type Jaguar.

'In fact, the Bullit is so much fun to drive that it would probably bore you all to recount its perfect balance whilst cornering on the limit.'

The Bullit was not sold as a kit; it was only available as a complete car. It came with uprated brakes (with Ferodo DS11 pads on the front), suspension modifications (Armstrong adjustables at the rear, a smaller-diameter front anti-roll bar, and bigger wheels/tyres), a two-tone paint job, better lighting, front spoiler (to fit this, the front bumper had to be removed), rear-window louvres, and a plethora of other goodies. If you couldn't run to the turbo engine, the braking, suspension, and cosmetic improvements were available for the 1600GT Capri.

Broadspeed continued to offer its famed Bullit conversions until the company's demise in 1980. At the tail end of the 1970s, the complete conversions (Broadspeed didn't believe in modifying the engine without modifying the chassis) cost around £2,600 and delivered in the region of 200bhp. Apparently Broadspeed did make one twin-turbo Capri.

Crayford

Crayford, better known for its well-engineered convertible and cabriolet conversions, was actually amongst the first to 'go large' with the Capri, the Crayford Eliminator predating Ford's own Capri V6. The Capri Exterminator was a 4.7-litre V8-engined 'Q' car first shown at the 1969 Motor Show. Spain was the biggest taker, with 30 cars being shipped to the company's Spanish distributor.

↓ ↓ **The last Crayford Exterminator. (Crayford Convertible Car Club)**

↓ **Very early Crayford Exterminator. (Crayford Convertible Car Club)**

↑ Photographed at Warley, this 1972 Capri 3000E features some unusual body modifications. The rear spoiler would appear on the Capri Special. (Ford Motor Company)

Janspeed

Janspeed's 2.8 Injection Turbo installation utilised all of the Capri's standard injection system but was mated to a modified engine management system. This was not a DIY conversion and was only sold on the basis of the work being done in Janspeed's workshops in Salisbury. It was a comprehensive package that also comprised a much stronger, cast exhaust manifold, a high-flowing Roto-Master RM60 turbocharger, a bespoke intercooler, an uprated radiator, and an oil cooler.

The turbo drew the air in via the standard flap valve, and then compressed it before pushing it through the intercooler. The cooled air was then routed back through the standard throttle butterfly. The beauty of this system was that there was a reserve of cooled air available, and throttle lag – often the bane of turbocharged installations – was almost entirely eliminated. To complete the conversion, Janspeed (a company famed for its quality performance exhaust manifolds and systems) also provided a low backpressure exhaust system. In 1984 the cost of the conversion was £1,750 plus VAT. Interestingly, the standard compression ratio was retained. Power was approximately 215bhp.

The company also marketed a kit for the 3.0 Essex V6. Unlike the 2.8i kit, this could be fitted by a competent DIYer. Janspeed insisted that the compression ratio be lowered and its preferred method was to machine a combustion chamber in the cylinder heads. The standard Weber carburettor was retained but suitably rejetted. A very well thought out conversion, it utilised a Roto-Master turbo on the nearside of the engine, with a pipe taking the exhaust charge from the other bank of cylinders and into a collector box beneath the turbo. The boost control was handled by a wastegate screwed into the original manifold (limited to 5psi), and there was a clever spacer between the exhaust manifold and the Weber. This allowed the pressurised air to circulate at all times and also for the provision of a pressure-sensitive switch (connected to the all-important fuel enrichment valve). Power was approximately 175bhp.

LuMo

LuMo, part of the Luton Motors Group, based in Dunstable, Bedfordshire, was famous for its LuMo Cortina 1600E TC, which, as its name suggests,

upgraded the brakes, cooling system, suspension, and the rear axle. Gearing was changed so that the car could take advantage of the increase in power to give it more relaxed cruising. Everything was done to the highest standards.

Race Proved went on to modify other Ford vehicles, including the Capri. Various Weslake-derived 'Comanche' tuning kits for the Capri were offered, with a choice of 170, 180, 190, and 220bhp engines. Top of the tuned Race Proved Capris was the mad as a hatter 'Stampede'. Fitted with a tuned 302 V8, it had 285bhp with which to terrify its driver, passengers, and anyone else who happened to be using the road at the time.

Super Speed

Formed by brothers Mike and John Young, and based in Ilford, Super Speed was a key player in the British Saloon Car Championship in the 1960s. Supported (but not in an official capacity) by Ford, the Super Speed Anglias were progressively developed into class-winning machines. In 1966, driven by Mike Young and Chris Craft, the Super

Speed Anglias saw off the works Mini Cooper Ss, winning the up to 1,300cc class ten times. Mike Young finished the season as class winner and fourth overall in the championship.

Although well known for its racing exploits, Super Speed was probably better known for its Ford tuning expertise and in particular its extremely well engineered and exciting Essex V6 engine transplants. During the late 1960s and throughout the 1970s the company transplanted V6 engines into a variety of Ford cars, including Anglias, Escorts, Cortinas, Corsairs and, of course, Capris. What was so good about Super Speed was that it didn't just drop in a V6. When you took your car to Super Speed you got the whole caboodle – suspension upgrade, brake improvements, cooling tweaks, etc – and the engine would also be positioned further back to get the weight distribution spot-on. And if the standard V6 was too tame for you, Super Speed also offered a range of tuning goodies.

If even a tuned V6 Capri proved to be too tame, Super Speed offered a Capri conversion that featured a 5.7-litre Mustang V8 with a monstrous 380bhp on tap.

↑ Super Speed was one of many Ford Tuning companies that cut its teeth on the Anglia, before moving on to the Escort and Capri.
(Ford Motor Company)

Turbo Technics

Founded in 1981 by Geoffrey Kershaw, Turbo Technics – based in Northampton – specialises in automotive turbochargers and associated turbo equipment. Such was the company's reputation in the early 1980s (and still is), that it offered two Ford-sanctioned conversions for the Capri 2.8i. The 200bhp conversion, which utilised a Garrett T3 turbo, special exhaust manifold with pulse separation, and special intercooler, ran the standard compression ratio and drove through the standard transmission, although the company advised that owners should upgrade the suspension and brakes. Turbo Technics also offered a 'Total Performance Package' that provided upgraded brakes, suspension, and transmission, and adjustable boost pressure. With the lowering of the compression ratio, and the raising of the boost pressure, power climbed to 230bhp. In this form the Capri would reach 60mph in 6.2 seconds and achieve 145mph flat out.

When the Capri 280 was launched, an agreement was reached with Ford whereby the 200bhp system was officially made available through the Ford dealership network with Ford promotion. Between 80 and 100 Capri 280s were converted.

Turbo Technics has recently relaunched the 200bhp kit, which is available for the capable DIYer. At the time of publication the cost was £2,500 plus VAT.

The Capri Mako

A German Capri with an American heart. Launched in the late 1970s, and the brainchild of former Ford racing chassis engineer Gerd Knözinger, the Mako V8 was quite some machine. Under the bonnet lay a 250bhp Boss 302 V8, which was topped off with a Solex copy of a Rochester Quadrajet (this was done to meet German emission standards). The V8 was mated to a toploader four-speed. The rear axle was more contemporary, as it came from a Mustang II. To gain the all-important TUV approval, Peugeot ventilated front discs were fitted, as were special

↓ **Turbo Technics Capri turbo installation. (Turbo Technics)**

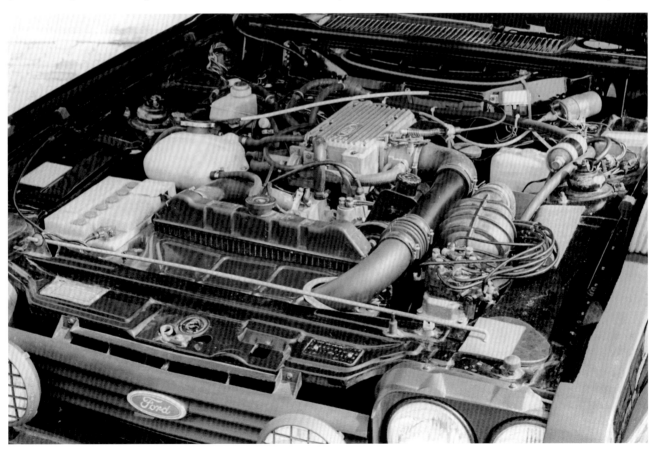

calipers and Mustang II rear drum brakes. A very well-engineered conversion, the Mako V8 would cover a standing quarter-mile in 15.3 seconds and run all the way to 148mph.

Open-air Capris

Probably with the export market (those with sunnier climes) in mind, Ford had given the matter of a convertible Capri some considerable thought. It even went as far as commissioning Coventry-based coachbuilder Carbodies to convert two Capris for them to evaluate. Carbodies had a long history of working with Ford, and the company produced the Consul, Zephyr, and Zodiac convertibles. Sadly, despite the promise it showed and its undoubted good looks, Ford didn't persevere with the convertible Capri project.

This left the way clear for other specialist companies/coachbuilders to create their own takes on the convertible Capri.

E.D. ABBOTT

E.D. Abbott of Farnham produced just nine convertible Capris. Their conversion was attractive and well executed.

CRAYFORD

By far the best-known and most popular convertible Capri was produced by Britain's foremost convertible and cabriolet specialist, Crayford. Based in Westerham, Kent, Crayford

↑ 1969 E.D. Abbott's open Capri at Dunton. (Ford Motor Company)

did development work for a number of major manufacturers, undertook estate and hatchback conversions, bullet-proofing and, of course, convertibles and cabriolets.

At the 1969 motor show Crayford launched its 'Caprice' convertible Capri, which was probably one of the company's most attractive conversions. Around 35 were sold. This was an attractive, if expensive, proposition. Much of the Capri's strength lay in its monocoque bodyshell, so removing the roof meant that much extra work had to be carried out in order to restore its rigidity. The extra cost reflected the amount of re-engineering required. Crayford were masters of this type of conversion and the cars are much sought-after.

↓ The Crayford Caprice. (Crayford Convertible Car Club)

CHAPTER 8
BUYING, OWNING AND RESTORING A CAPRI

Regrettably, not long after it ceased production the Capri seemed to drift into automotive obscurity. From being a car with masses of street appeal, a no-nonsense ability, and blessed with a simple yet affable nature, the Capri spent years in the motoring wilderness. In a short space of time its status altered dramatically. This former macho mini-muscle car was soon perceived to be at best a cheap runabout and, at worst, an old banger. Once coveted, the Capri became an automotive pariah. The mighty had indeed fallen, and for a good number of years there seemed to be no signs to indicate that the Capri would regain its past status.

There were exceptions, of course. The RS2600 and RS3100 models have always been regarded as collectable, but the classic car movement tended to brush all other Capris aside. Even the motoring public seemed to regard the Capri as a yesterday's car. Perhaps this was because during the 1980s there were those critics (including some of Ford's hierarchy) who were constantly trying to draw a line under the Capri. They regarded this former front-runner as a relic of a previous age, and they let their feelings and observations be known. Mud sticks!

The old adage that 'any publicity is good publicity' didn't work for the Capri. Criticism, negativity, disapproval, the Capri was subjected to all this and more during its final years. Of course, when something has no perceived status, no significant monetary value, and is largely overlooked, it becomes a victim … a victim of circumstance and breakers' yards. The really sad thing about the Capri's fall from grace is that a huge number met an untimely, unnecessary, and unpleasant end in the jaws of a crusher.

But the Capri is a hugely important car. An icon. For decades it was part of the British psyche, an emotional reference point. Mercifully, in more recent times the motoring community has recognised that the Capri truly deserves its classic status, and there are numerous specialist companies dedicated to its preservation and promotion.

The Capri is a genuinely accessible and easy-to-own classic. Better still, the virtues with which it was blessed when in production – affordability, reliability, ease of maintenance, good handling, good performance, tuneability – still hold true today. In fact, considering the uniformity of design and the benign and oft-characterless nature of many of today's mainstream cars, the Capri's distinctive shape, classic rear-wheel drive, and pure unadulterated connectivity with the driver makes a more persuasive case for itself now than it did in its heyday.

There is no doubt that the Capri is in the ascendancy. Having spent far too long out of the limelight, in recent years it has finally become recognised for the affordable, attractive, capable, and exciting sports coupe it always has been. The Capri is a genuinely practical classic. Often imitated but never bettered, the Capri didn't break the mould, it created it.

Which Capri?

MK1 AND FACELIFT

There is absolutely no doubting the fact that the Mk1 and facelift Capris are the most collectable and most sought-after – the earlier the better, in fact. The RS2600 and RS3100 in particular have always scored when it comes to desirability and collectability. The RS models fetch serious money, even for examples that are well past their prime. Many parts unique to the model are almost impossible to find. Genuine Mk1 rear lights can be as much as £700, new front wings are £1,500 a pair, and quarter-bumpers are only available second-hand. Fortunately a good number of the decals have been remanufactured, and mechanical parts are not a problem. A good daily driver

← Capri 3000 GXL partway through restoration. (Dave Hurst)

↑ **If you're very lucky you might be able to pick up a nice RS2600. (Ford Motor Company)**

RS3100 can be had for £6–8,000, but unmolested or well-restored cars can command £15,000, with some exceptional cars changing hands for much more – concours cars that have the original bodyshell and panels can fetch as much as £20,000. Remember, the RS2600 was never officially imported but if you're prepared to travel, and can cope with a left-hooker, there are plenty of survivors to choose from.

Genuine RS3100s have chassis numbers that start with BBECND. Never consider buying one of these cars without first contacting clubs such as the AVO Owners' Club and the RS Owners' Club. There is a wealth of knowledge within these clubs and they'll make you aware of the plusses and the pitfalls. They'll also help ensure that the car you buy is genuine and not a replica. It's essential not only to ensure that the car is a pukka item, but also to check that it's structurally and mechanically sound. Basket cases have been restored to concours condition (more on this anon), but this is not a job for the faint-hearted, fiscally challenged, or mechanically inept. It is advisable to enlist the help of an expert when viewing. The same goes for all Capri purchases, really.

And it's not just the RS models that are collectable. Any early car is – it's just that they won't inflict as much damage on your wallet! The Mk1 1600GT, especially in XLR trim, is highly desirable, as are any of the 3.0-litre V6 versions. A 1300GT would certainly generate a great deal of interest (even more so if it was an XLR). Even a base model 1300, in good condition, has its plusses. Indeed, all early models are worthy of consideration, although it has to be said that the V4 models are less favoured.

Original trim parts are hard to find, although companies such as Aldridge Trimming have a wide range of very high-quality replacement trim for the Mk1, and its Capri range is regularly being added to. It's the trim that gives each particular variant its unique identity. Headlinings are almost invariably likely to have suffered from cracks, tears, and staining from cigarette smoke. Genuine Ford headlining material from this period is virtually non-existent. Specialist trimmers will be able to replace it in a better material, but it won't be original.

Ford stopped making trim parts very shortly after production of each model ended, which means that interior trim is exceptionally hard to

track down. The same applies to the exterior trim.
Bumpers, badges, handles, headlights, rear lights
(especially on facelift models) can be very, very hard
to find. Look to see if it's carrying its full compliment
of badges etc. Heated rear windows can fail so check
this and make sure that all window seals are in good
order. It's possible to get replacements, but leaking
seals are invariably a route to rotten metalwork.
Always replace a toughened windscreen with a
laminated one.

Check the condition of the seats, fronts in
particular. The seat structure could be in a poor
state and the reclining/adjusting mechanisms can
succumb to age and/or weight! If seat belts are
fitted, look for evidence of fraying, damaged buckles,
and rust around the mounting points.

Unless you plan to seriously modify the car
(which, given the rarity of the early models, is a
heinous crime), you should be looking to retain its
period charm. With any early Capri, the keyword
is originality. The more complete and authentic the
car is, the more value it has. As already mentioned,
certain trim items and body parts are exceptionally
difficult to locate. Bear this in mind when purchasing.
Some parts, even relatively small and seemingly
insignificant ones, fetch eye-watering prices. Period
tuned cars such as the LuMo, Savage, Broadspeed,
etc are harder to price. Good examples will usually
command high prices, but they still shouldn't break
the bank. The Capri Special is also worthy of
consideration.

CAPRI II

The Capri II has gained something of an unenviable
and unjustified reputation. Straddling the era
between the iconic MkI and the well-specced and
more refined Capri III, the Capri II tends to be
regarded as the 'unloved' Capri. This is rather unfair.
The Capri II has many good qualities and is a more
available and more affordable purchase than either
the MkI or the Capri III.

As with all Fords of this era, parts interchangeability
is second to none, and the Capri II is a car that has
found favour with the modifiers. It's simple to swap,
substitute, and change parts, from engines to trim.
All S models are highly desirable, although it's very
easy to create a clone. If you're passionate about
authenticity, check the car ... and the paperwork.
The JPS-inspired variants will always command higher
prices. Decals are available, but trim is becoming very

← Parts for early Capris
are hard to source. Check
the condition of the
bumpers, lights, driving
lamps, overriders, etc.
(John Colley Photography)

↑ ← Check the condition
of interior and exterior
trim and any extras that
might have been fitted.
(John Colley Photography)

↑ The Capri II
– sometimes overlooked,
but a very good car indeed.
(Ford Motor Company)

→ Pace, grace, and a
reasonable amount of
space: the Capri 2.8i.
(Ford Motor Company)

hard to obtain. Indeed, original trim parts and panels are becoming scarce for all versions, although Aldridge has remanufactured some items.

It was during Capri II production that the famous X-pack conversions were introduced. Valuing X-pack Capris is an inexact science. Nevertheless, good examples will always command a premium. Again,

it's relatively easy to create a replica, as GRP panels are still manufactured by Fibresports. However, unless you want a car with a genuine X-pack provenance, don't be put off. Just make certain that the conversion has been undertaken properly and that the GRP body panels aren't covering rotten metalwork.

CAPRI III

There are still plenty of Capri IIIs available and they make for a very good and very useable classic. The Laser, especially the 2.0-litre version, is a very astute buy, as are any of the S versions. Of course, this was the period when Ford flooded the market with special editions. So with any of the Cabaret, Calypso, and GT4 versions you should be aiming for originality. All of these (especially the GT4) are interesting and make for a welcome change from the norm. Condition, especially as regards interior trim, is vital.

The Capri 2.8i and Injection Special are exceptionally good cars, and the 280 is thought by many to be the ultimate everyday Capri. Once again, look at the condition of the interior trim. Even the leather-covered Recaro seats are not immune to wear. Fortunately there are specialist companies who will re-cover the seats to a very high standard.

There is no doubt that the Tickford Capri is an extremely desirable car. It turns heads and eats miles. It's not a particularly difficult car to live with either – provided that it's been looked after properly. Tickfords fetch serious money, so thoroughly investigate its provenance and service history. As with any exclusive and desirable high-performance Capri, if it doesn't have the paperwork to back it up and doesn't feel right, then walk away!

Mechanical: engines

V4 COLOGNE
1,298cc, 1,488cc, 1,688cc, and 1,993cc

The V4 engine, especially the 1,993cc version, has always had a poor reputation, although it has not always been deserving of it. Typical problems are head gasket woes, oil leaks, noisy valve gear, and failing oil pumps. Check to see what has been done to the car, when, and by whom. The fibre teeth on the timing gears tend to strip after high mileages. The only cure is to fit steel timing gear – noisy but reliable! Balance-shaft bearings can wear out, as can the valve gear. Check for oil leaks too.

↑ **Until the 3-litre V6 arrived, the 2-litre V4 engine was top of the range.**

IN-LINE FOUR-CYLINDER KENT
1,298cc and 1,599cc

The 1300 and 1600 Kent engines are a byword for reliability and tuneability. True, they're not immune to neglect, poor maintenance, and high mileage, but they're simple and easy-to-fix engines that give fantastic service. Just do the usual checks for oil leaks, head gasket leaks, timing chain rattle, and piston wear. Piston/bore wear is highlighted by the engine's thirst for oil and fumes venting from the breather. Sometimes what appears to be a head gasket problem (oil in water and water in oil) is actually the result of a cracked block, which has probably happened after an overenthusiastic rebore. Liners can be fitted but a replacement block is a better bet. 711M blocks are expensive and rare.

IN-LINE FOUR-CYLINDER PINTO
1,593cc and 1,993cc

Post-1972 Capri 1600s were fitted with the 'small' Pinto. If it's a high-mileage unit, then oil leaks are likely to be prevalent (especially from the cambox

gasket). Quality oil and regular oil changes are essential on this engine, otherwise the oil feed pipe and spray bar will block and severe camshaft and cam follower wear will occur. Listen for the telltale dry-sounding tapping. If wear is evident, the whole lot will need to be replaced, which necessitates the removal of the cylinder head. Timing belts are not a recognised failure point, although fitting a new belt kit at regular intervals is a sensible precaution. Fitting an aftermarket Weber carburettor in place of the Ford VV item results in smoother running and better fuel economy.

The 2.0-litre Pinto arrived with the Capri II and in many ways it's the definitive Capri power unit. It's a very good engine but can suffer from exactly the same problems as its 1600 sibling. Nonetheless, properly maintained this is widely regarded as one of the best engines ever produced by Ford, and a great choice for the Capri. It has massive spares availability, incredible tuning potential, and there are plenty available.

↑ **Although not as good as its bigger brother, the 'small' Pinto was a reasonable and workmanlike engine. (Ford Motor Company)**

→ **RS2600 power – Ford's first production fuel-injected engine. (Ford Motor Company)**

V6 COLOGNE

1,999cc, 2,294cc, 2,520cc, 2,637cc (RS2600), and 2,792cc

As fitted to the Capri III (and to German and American Capris). Although closely related to the V4, the V6 versions have fewer problems. Overtightening of the belt will cause premature failure of the water pump bearings, and the pump has been known to crack if the bolts are overtightened. The carburettor will invariably suffer after high mileage, so budget for a replacement or an overhaul. The Bosch fuel injection system is typically long-lasting and reliable. The system needs to be in good order, however, otherwise economy and performance will suffer. And it's expensive to fix. If the engine lacks its characteristic smoothness, then it's likely that the fuel filters need renewing and/or the high-pressure pump needs replacing. The fuel system needs to be surgically clean. Run fuel treatment through it as part of the regular servicing schedule and every so often fill the tank with premium petrol. In fact, the fuel system cleaner and quality petrol will reap long-term benefits on any engine.

V6 ESSEX

2,994cc and 3,091cc (RS3100)

The V6 Essex suffers from some of the same issues that afflict the Cologne V4 (although it doesn't have the balance-shafts). However, there's better availability of parts for this engine, and over the years Ford ironed out many of its inherent problems. There was also a big specialist market for it, and it can be found in numerous Marcos, Gilbern, TVR, and Reliant models, and many similar applications.

For many, many years the Essex V6 was the specialist sports car manufacturers' engine of choice. Plus, unlike the V4, which was given scant attention by Ford, the V6 was subject to an almost continuous run of factory development. Better still, a good number of specialist companies have followed a similar but more bespoke route. If you're a fan of vee-configuration engines, then a good V6 Essex provides serious performance, reasonable economy, and a glorious soundtrack … you know it makes sense! And it's eminently tuneable.

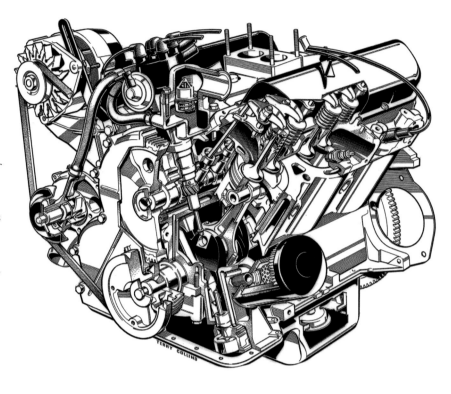

↑ **An all-time great – the lusty Essex V6. (Ford Motor Company)**

TURBOCHARGED

Turbocharged conversions (Turbo Technics, Janspeed, Allard, etc) were quite popular, and gave the Capri supercar performance. But the youngest Capri is now 23 years old and age will have taken its toll. However well converted the engine was, turbocharging does place it under extra stress. Check the water for signs of oil residue, look at the intercooler and hoses for splits, listen for unusual noises, and investigate the set-up (including hoses) thoroughly. Turbocharged engines require regular oil and filter changes and absolutely top-quality oil. 'Coking' can occur within the turbo if run at extreme temperatures, or if the engine has been shut down too quickly when very hot. Check for bearing wear (take off the inlet hose and wiggle the impellor – there should be no movement). And, with any turbocharged car, buy with your head and not your heart! The same approach should also be adopted when considering a Tickford.

Mechanical: gearboxes

MKI

The gearbox and axles are pretty much bulletproof and very well catered for in terms of spares if need arises. The rod-change mechanisms can become sloppy after lots of miles, the bearings can succumb to use and/or lack of oil, and the synchros (particularly second gear) can also weaken. Listen for propshaft and differential wear. Adopt a learner driver on/off throttle approach and you'll soon hear if there's any wear in the drivetrain or if there's a tendency to jump out of gear. Often it's not the gearbox bearings that are worn, it's the wheel bearings.

Autos (Borg-Warner Type 35 three-speed) are usually long-lived too. You'll occasionally find an auto mated to a four-cylinder engine, but most are typically partnered with the lustier V6 versions. Autos should change up and down smoothly and all gears should be present and correct – don't forget to try reverse! The transmission fluid should be clean and it should also smell like oil. If the oil exhibits an unpleasant odour, and/or is swimming with dark-coloured particles, then it's a fair bet that the transmission's been overheated.

CAPRI II

Manual gearboxes and drivetrain are pretty much as per the MkI. Ford fitted its very tough C3 automatic gearbox in place of the Borg-Warner Type 35.

CAPRI III

Early 2.8 Injections had the four-speed gearbox, which although not as good for high-speed cruising had a slicker change than the five-speeder and was quicker off the mark too. Neither the four- nor five-speed gearboxes are problematic, although check for worn synchromesh (especially on the hard-used second gear) and noisy bearings. Also listen out for a noisy propshaft and differential (the LSD on the Special and 280 is always a touch 'musical', but it shouldn't be overly so). Post-1983 all 2.0-litres, 2.8-litres, and a handful of 1600s left the factory with five-speed gearboxes. Three 280 automatics are known of, although these are likely to have been converted by dealers.

Mechanical: steering, suspension, brakes

ALL MODELS

All Capris, from 1969 to 1986, can suffer from the same basic problems. Look for worn suspension and anti-roll bar bushes, worn track control arms, ineffective or leaking dampers/struts, broken coil springs, sagging leaf springs, sloppy steering, leaks on cars fitted with PAS, kerbed and/or corroded alloys, warped discs (brake discs are unique on the RS3100, but some owners have converted to a 2.8i set-up), grabbing/sticky calipers, fluid leaks, ineffectual servos, corroded brake pipes, etc. MkI 3.0-litre Capris did have a tendency to weave under braking. Look to see if the hydraulic pipe runs to each wheel are the same length. The good news is that all of the mechanical items are a relatively easy and affordable fix, and there are plenty of uprated replacement components available.

Bodywork

ALL MODELS

Structurally, the Capri is little different to any of its contemporaries, and in all honesty unless it's been subject to a recent, extensive, and exceptionally good restoration (and there are a good number of such cars out there) you're unlikely to find a totally rust-free example. Broadly speaking, the MkI, Capri II, and Capri III all suffer in the same places (although the Capri II and III have the hatchback, of course, which will also rot through if a poor seal allows the ingress of water).

The wings (especially the fronts) are capable of holding vast quantities of mud, road grime, road salt, etc, and if they do they'll crumble away in time. The bad news is that originals are incredibly hard to find. Thankfully, specialist companies (Ex-Pressed Steel Panels, for example) have a huge range of repair/replacement sections for the MkI and Capri II/III. Where replacements are simply not available (RS3100) the only course of action is to repair. This means removing the door, as the wing has to be welded along the rear edge too. There are no issues as far as replacement glass is concerned, although it makes

Checklist of areas to investigate

- The front valance
- The area around the headlamps
- The joins between each wing and the lower valance
- The stiffeners between the top rear section of the wheelarch edges and inner wings
- The bonnet edge
- Where the inner wing meets up with the outer wing
- MacPherson strut top mounts (these must be thoroughly investigated for signs of rust and/or botched repairs)
- Seat-belt mounting points
- Inner wings
- Chassis rails
- Wing tops
- Bulkhead
- Screen pillars
- Door pillars
- Door bottoms
- Sills (inner and outer)
- The box sections behind the front/rear wheels
- The longitudinal box sections
- The cross-member (particularly where the anti-roll bar mounts attach to it)
- Rear spring hangers
- Jacking points (look for signs of botched repairs)
- Rear arches
- Floorpans
- Boot well
- The vinyl roof (check for signs of rust bubbles beneath the vinyl)
- Everywhere, in fact!

sense to replace a toughened windscreen with a laminated one.

Don't be too dismayed by what you find, however. With time, money, and expertise just about any Capri, even the proverbial basket case, can be salvaged, whatever its condition. You just have to decide if the car justifies this kind of investment. The RS models certainly do, as does any rare Capri variant, and just about every MkI (not that I'm biased, of course). Often the restoration process will require a huge amount of detective work, the patience of a saint, the skills of a master craftsman, and the riches of Croesus, but the end result will be worth it.

Help and advice

The Capri enthusiast clubs (see Appendix) are very good in a number of respects. They offer a great social scene and should be your first port of call for advice. And they're incredibly useful in sourcing parts. Some members often have multiple spares, which they're willing to let go if they know it's to help someone with a restoration. The Capri Internet forums (see Appendix) can also be a fantastic source of advice and help.

Body restoration

Like all types of repair work, structural repairs should only be carried out by a competent person. There's no doubt that we live in a society that's seemingly overburdened with health and safety regulations, but in the case of car maintenance and repair good and safe working practice is essential. Always follow manufacturers' instructions, always use the right equipment or tools for the job, always wear protective clothing and eye gear when required, and always ensure that the car is safely mounted on its supports (axle stands, ramps, etc). Never cut corners. Store flammable materials, welding bottles and the like safely. If in doubt, use RCD safety adaptors when using electrical equipment. All garages or workshops should have a fire extinguisher that's up to date and accessible.

If you're in any doubt about your abilities to tackle any aspect of your Capri's restoration, take the car to a professional. The Capri is well catered for and the owners' clubs and forums will point you in the right direction. However, before committing yourself to any specialist arrange to see some of the projects in which they've been involved and try to speak to the owners of the cars. With any restoration, there will be the inevitable nasties that are uncovered along the way, and these will

↑ **Wheelarch and rear quarter-panel repair sections. (Dave Hurst)**

↗ **Wheelarch and rear quarter-panel repair under way. (Dave Hurst)**

↓ → **Chassis rail repairs and underside partway through restoration. (Dave Hurst)**

add to the duration of the build and the expense. Nevertheless, you should discuss a ballpark cost for the job, and preferably split the project into stages. Insist on regular updates and, if possible, a photographic record of the rebuild.

Capri 3000GXL restoration

The following photographs were taken by Dave Hurst during the restoration of his 3000GXL. They're just a small sample, but they serve to illustrate what one can expect to uncover during a typical restoration and how the repairs can be undertaken.

'And here's one I made earlier. …'

When Dave Hurst bought RPU 655M, a 1973 RS3100, it was the proverbial basket case and

→ Boot floor cut out
and chassis rails repaired.
(Dave Hurst)

→ New spare wheel well
fitted, boot floor repaired,
inner wings repaired.
(Dave Hurst)

→ Boot repaired, new rear
panel and valance fitted.
(Dave Hurst)

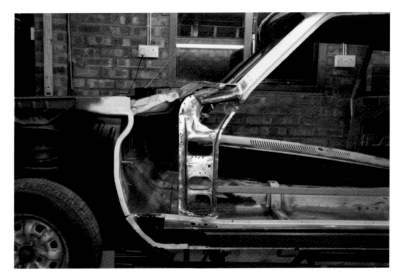

↑ Repairs under way to inner wing, B post, and sills. (Dave Hurst)

↑ Rustproofing under way. (Dave Hurst)　　↓ New 'old stock' panel fitted. (Dave Hurst)

much worse than the 3000GXL he is currently working on. Nevertheless it was still his dream car, as he explains: 'I'd always wanted an RS3100 and all I could really afford was a restoration project. RPU 655M was in a very poor condition, but it was a Spa Special, had the right VIN plate, and the original engine. It was also one of the Ford-owned cars that area sales managers took around the dealers in an attempt to boost sales.'

Had it not been an RS3100, in all honesty, RPU 655M should have been scrapped. It was in a dire state. Although Ford dealers offered rust-proofing in the 1970s, few owners ever took up this option. This, coupled with the fact that in the 1970s no car maker contemplated eliminating rust traps, meant that the Capri rotted away quickly, RS badge or not! Dave knew he'd bought a rotten car, but he was up for a challenge.

As he works in the nuclear power industry, as a maintenance technician, Dave's no stranger to the angle grinder, or any other piece of workshop equipment for that matter. He wasn't a restoration virgin either. 'I got into body restoration with a 3000GT I owned,' he elaborates, 'and after I finished this I enrolled on a 14-week restoration evening class in my local college. When I'd finished restoring the 3000GT, I took it to show the tutors. They were bowled over and suggested that I do a day-release course.'

Dave did more than that – in his spare time he took numerous other courses and in the process he gained his City & Guilds Body Repair Level 3, and City & Guilds Paint and Refinishing Level 3, and was voted vehicle bodyshop 'Student of the Year'. College proved to be a revelation for Dave and he learnt many other restoration skills. As a bonus, when he was restoring the RS3100 he was able to use some of the college's facilities, such as the jig system and spray booth. Dave undertook each and every part of the build. This even included making machine tools from scratch and pressing out the panels that were impossible to obtain, all the mechanical work, and the painting.

Of course, not everyone would relish such a challenge, have the necessary skills, and be able to access such specialist equipment. But RPU 655M shows just what can be achieved. Over a period of five years (of evenings and weekends) Dave turned RPU 655M from rusty relic to concours Capri. Wonderful!

← Dave Hurst single-handedly turned a sad, neglected, and exceptionally rusty Capri RS3100 from this ...
(Dave Hurst)

↓ ... to this very solid concours one.
(CTP Studios)

CHAPTER 9
MODIFYING THE CAPRI

As with modifying any car, it's imperative to ensure that the structure of the car is sound. There's absolutely no point in spending money on upgrading the suspension if the bodyshell has seen better days. Ensure that the spring hangars, MacPherson strut top plates, anti-roll bar mountings/bushes, TCA and leaf-spring bushes etc are in good order. Then it's a matter of horses for courses really. Before you do the upgrade, you really need to decide what it is you intend doing with your Capri – ie fast road car, occasional track day use, serious track day use, or competition. Oh … don't forget, you will need to make your insurance company aware of the modifications you've undertaken.

Suspension, brakes, tyres

FAST ROAD
The first step along the road to handling nirvana involves fitting a set of top-quality McPherson struts/inserts and dampers (eg Gaz, Bilstein, Spax, AVO, or Koni). Even if you do nothing else to the chassis, this will transform the handling and improve the ride quality. When combined with uprated/lowered front springs (spring rates will depend on the weight of the engine fitted, but 145lb is ideal for most people, with 170lb being the maximum), 1in lowering blocks at the rear, uprated suspension bushes (polybushes preferably), uprated anti-roll bar bushes, etc, the Capri becomes a surprisingly nimble and controllable car. If the rear dampers are adjustable, don't set them too hard. Just a few clicks will suffice to render the rear end less prone to road irregularities and much better in the wet. It's also worth investing in an axle location kit (such as the Caprisport item) or the tried and tested Watt's linkage system. Tyre pressures are also important. These will depend on the tyres, of course, but a

good starting point is 28psi all round with 32psi being the maximum.

That's really it as far as road use goes. If you modify the suspension any further the ride will become harsh; there will be much more road noise evident, and the shock loadings will feed into the structure far more violently.

The front brakes do over 80% of the work. Good quality discs, a set of fast road pads (eg EBC Green Stuff), and braided brake lines will improve the braking and pedal feel. It's best to fit new discs as well as pads and the pads/lining must be fitted in pairs. Vented (and grooved/cross-drilled) discs work very well on the Capri, but you'll need suitable calipers or to invest in a caliper widening kit. At the rear, just fit a set of quality linings. You can fit rear discs, but unless you have a seriously powerful car it's not worth the cost or effort.

Brake fluid is hydroscopic and over a period of time the moisture content will rise. Change it every two years and only refill with the correct DOT-rated fluid. Never use racing brake fluid on the road. Check the condition of the brakes' pipes/hoses.

Tyre choice is exceptionally important. It's utterly pointless uprating the suspension if your Capri is rolling along on some spurious brand of tyre. Always fit a premium branded tyre, of the right width for the wheel, and ensure that they're E-marked and have the correct speed rating. Don't mix patterns if at all possible, and certainly don't fit different pattern tyres on the same axle. Good tyres transform the Capri, as they will work harmoniously with the suspension modifications. Don't forget to get the tracking/alignment reset after any suspension work.

OCCASIONAL TRACK DAY
Circuit driving is not at all like driving on the road. The speeds are significantly faster and the loadings imposed on the suspension can be enormous. On the front, you need to be thinking about shorter,

← **Ultra wide-bodied (FAT) Capri with supercharged Rover V8. (David Morgan Jones)**

↑ **Getting serious! This particular Caprisport conversion uses uprated and adjustable platform front struts, Brembo four-pot calipers, and 300mm vented/cross-drilled discs.** (Caprisport)

↑ ↑ **Caprisport's impressive 315 kit.** (Caprisport)

stiffer (195lb) front springs, with 1.5in lowering blocks and stiffer leaf springs at the rear. Don't go too stiff or too low at the rear as this will upset the handling, stability, and traction. Strut and damper rates will need to be increased, and you need to ensure that the amount of travel is sufficient. Struts/dampers that bottom out will not only be damaged, but the handling will also go seriously awry. A front strut brace is always a good idea, although if you're running certain carburettor set-ups you'll have to check that it will clear. Pushed hard on a track the Capri will understeer, so to eradicate this tendency you'll need more negative camber at the front. This means investing in modified track control arms and steering arm spacers. An axle location kit is a must.

Vented and grooved/cross-drilled discs are also a must, as are better calipers. However, if you provide the front end with too much stopping power you'll need to address the balance of the system. This will entail the fitment of a bias-system, and you'll also have to dispense with the servo (or fit an additional servo). There is another option, however. Fit an adjustable pressure valve in the main line to the rear brakes and you can tailor the braking pressure to suit. Even if you're still running 13in wheels, it's possible to fit 260/265mm discs (make sure that you check with the manufacturer first, though, as there is usually a minimum wheel diameter requirement). Kits are available that come complete with brackets, pipes, four-pot calipers, and uprated pads. Mondeo and Granada-based kits are available. Larger brake calipers invariably means fitting a larger master cylinder and larger servo(s). Speak to the supplier to make sure that you get the right parts. Whatever set-up you choose, don't opt

for a pad compound that's too hard, as they'll take time to reach their proper operating temperature. A medium compound is more than adequate.

You really need to invest in a set of wheels/tyres specifically for track use. The wheels will need to have the correct offset and make sure that you don't run into clearance issues. Track day tyres (such as Toyo 888) will be biased towards outright grip, and the reduction in lap times, the poise of the chassis, and braking distances will be improved remarkably. For those 'occasional' inclement days you'll need to have a set of wet-weather tyres. As the temperature won't be as high, a set of top-quality performance road tyres should suffice if your budget won't run to pukka wets. Tyre pressures need to be much higher, so you have to discuss this with the manufacturer's technical department; you'll need to talk about suitable rim sizes too.

Before you commit to track day events, go and spectate. Wander around the paddock, chat to owners, and ask to see what they've done to their cars.

REGULAR TRACK DAY

If you're becoming serious about track days, and you're pushing your Capri very hard, you'll need a bigger anti-roll bar and 220lb springs on the front. In reality you'll not have to go any harder than 165lb at the rear. If you want to go stiffer on the front you need to invest in a set of coilovers (300lb springs should be the maximum). A 2in suspension drop is as low as you should go. The rear end definitely needs restraining so think along the lines of a proper four-, five-, or six-link conversion. The good old Watt's linkage still does a great job of work.

For dry-weather use, wider and lower profile tyres are a good investment but they will put more strain on the suspension/wheel bearings etc. Fitting larger-diameter wheels (16in is the sensible maximum) enables you to fit bigger brakes, and to be able to choose from a wider range of tyres.

On the front, the brakes can be uprated to 280mm, 300mm and beyond (but only if you're using larger diameter-wheels). If you want to run 315mm front discs, you'll require 16in wheels. Rear disc brake conversions are available and they must be fitted if you are using 280mm front discs and above. If you don't, you just lock the front wheels, especially in the wet. And always use

rear calipers on the rear. Due to their design, and rating, front calipers will only work properly on the front. Having fitted rear discs you'll probably need to get the handbrake cable extended too. Again, contact the brake kit manufacturers. Pad compounds needn't be too hard and this will also depend on the type of discs/calipers you've fitted. Oh … certain performance calipers don't have dust seals fitted. If you use your car on the road, these calipers are not suitable, as premature wear will occur.

COMPETITION

This will depend on the type of championship you want to participate in. Before modifying your Capri, speak to the organisers and scrutinise the regulations very, very thoroughly. There is nothing worse than spending the winter preparing your car, only to have it thrown out by the scrutineer!

ROLL-CAGES

Whilst it's possible to do track days in a car that doesn't have a roll-cage, it makes sense to have one fitted professionally. There are numerous companies that fabricate and fit roll-cages and

they'll be only too pleased to quote a price. You can, of course, get roll-cages as DIY kits but this type of work should only be undertaken by a competent person. There are simple six-point devices, multipoint, bolt-in, weld-in, and so on. The minimum type of protection you should entertain for track day use is the rear rollover hoop/cage. However, a full cage is a much better bet, especially if it's properly integrated into the structure of the car. If the car is also used on the road, check with your insurer. Most take a dim view of roll-cages, thinking that a car equipped thus will be driven in a much more spirited manner!

Engine

KENT

The Kent crossflow/pre-crossflow engine has been around almost since the dawn of motoring! It's a hugely responsive unit and you can tune it from mild to wild.

The crossflow engine arrived with the Cortina Mk2 and differs from the pre-crossflow by having the carburettor on the left and the exhaust on the

↑ Performance tyres such as Toyo Proxes 4 make all the difference …
(Martyn Morgan Jones)

↑ ↑ From mild to wild, the Capri can be just the car you want it to be.
(Ford Motor Company)

↑ The right design of wheel can really add to the Capri's appeal, 2.8 Pepperpot above and Minilite right. (David Morgan Jones; Gary Hawkins Photography)

right – hence crossflow. Also, the combustion chamber was in the piston (bowl in piston), although early heads featured a small combustion chamber. Crossflow engines were fitted to Mk1 and Mk2 Escorts, Mk2 and Mk3 Cortinas, and some transits. In 1970 the block was changed to the thick-walled 711M, which featured square mains caps and a modified crank seal.

Early blocks bore the casting marks 681F. You'll find the X/Flow fitted to Mk1/2 Escorts, Mk2/3 Cortinas, Mk1/2 Capris plus late Transits. The 1600 block is 7/16in taller than the 1300. Most cars came with a single choke Ford VV carb, although the 1.3 and 1.6 GT models had a 32/36 DGV Weber twin choke. Weber does a nice replacement manual choke carburettor, the 34ICH. On any engine that's still running points and condenser, it makes sense to fit a Lumenition or Aldon electronic ignition kit. This cuts down the servicing time and means that the engine runs more smoothly and more efficiently.

FAST ROAD

Kents are relatively easy to tune to GT spec, which usually means the biggest capacity block, slightly bigger valves (usually taken care of with a performance head), GT cam/fast road camshaft, free flow exhaust, and twin choke Weber. With these modifications you should see around 80–90bhp. Switch to a hotter camshaft and the power will jump to over 100bhp. To ensure reliability, stronger rod bolts should be used and the front pulley should be a one-piece steel item. The valve train needs to be strengthened with steel posts, spacers, and rocker shaft to cope with the

additional stresses caused by high-lift cams, heavy-duty valve springs, and increased revs. A double timing chain kit should also be fitted for the same reasons. Performance heads are available in both iron and brand new aluminium. All can be ordered with unleaded seats, which is advisable.

Longer duration camshafts with less lift can be very effective, but the current crop of high-lift, short duration camshafts are much better for the environment and perform just as well.

Various cast and forged pistons are available, and the block can be overbored. With +0.090 pistons, the capacity will be 1,696cc.

FASTER ROAD/MILD COMPETITION

Fit a stage 2 head, higher-lift camshaft, and get the Weber re-jetted (with final adjustment being undertaken on a rolling road), and you'll probably have in the region of 120bhp. You might be able to find a special Lynx manifold and this allows a single Weber 40 DCOE to be fitted. This set-up gives very good results. Swap the single Weber for twin 40 DCOE Webers and the power will climb to around 130bhp (you'll have to fit a side exit distributor cap to clear the inlet manifold). Even in this stage of tune, the car will be driveable and return reasonable economy when not being worked in anger.

SERIOUS COMPETITION

A stage 3 head, race camshaft, forged pistons, and twin 40 DCOE Webers will deliver up to 145bhp depending on the other components fitted. You'll have to give some serious thought to the ignition, which needs to be electronic. A matched distributor is a worthwhile investment. At this stage of tune many people swap to twin 45 DCOE Webers, although the resultant lower gas speed and less low-down torque means that this set-up is not ideal for hillclimb or rally use. If regulations allow it, a change to throttle bodies and mapped ignition, although not cheap, will reap dividends in torque and driveability. Generally speaking the safe maximum for a properly built engine is 7,500–8,000rpm.

Beyond this level of power (it's possible to get 185bhp+ from the Kent) you'll need to budget for steel rods, crank, special flywheel, and a full-race head.

Ford are now starting to reproduce the Kent engine in the USA back to its original spec, mainly for Formula Ford, but it will be available to the general public this year.

PINTO

FAST ROAD

Dating back to 1970, the Pinto is a belt-drive OHC engine with massive tuning potential and spares availability. For the 1.6 engines it's best to limit the modification to a free-flow air filter, fast road camshaft, and possibly a less restrictive tailbox. These should liberate around 10bhp. When changing the camshaft on any Pinto it's best to fit the complete kit, with new followers, new spray bar, and adjustable vernier.

If you're serious about tuning then it's best to ignore the 1.6 and move on up to the 2.0-litre. The crank is enormously strong but the early rods are only safe to 6,500rpm. Sierra 'injection' rods are wider and stronger and can run to 7,500rpm. The Sierra Injection '205' block is the tuner's favourite as it can accommodate the 2.1-litre conversion with ease. However, if you don't use pistons that are specially produced for this conversion then the block will need decking, the rod journals have to be narrowed, and if the head's been skimmed you'll need to have the compression ratio and valve to piston clearances checked.

The 2.0-litre head features massive ports and it will really respond to better carburation. However, at this stage the 32/36 DGAV Weber is more than capable. Coupled with a stage I head and

↓ **Modified Pinto with twin Webers, strut brace, etc. (David Morgan Jones)**

a fast road camshaft, the DGAV will flow enough to produce a lusty 135bhp. Whilst all this work is going on, it's wise to have the head professionally converted for unleaded (injection heads already are, of course).

FASTER ROAD/MILD COMPETITION

Take the head to stage 2, fit a hotter camshaft, bolt on a pair of suitably jetted 45 DCOE Webers, add a free-flow exhaust system, and you should be getting a solid 150bhp, possibly more. The head should really be fitted with proper valve guides in place of the standard cast-in variety. Downdraft 44IDF Webers can be used instead of the 45 DCOEs, but they're very expensive … nice though!

SERIOUS COMPETITION

This is where you need to be considering steel rods, forged pistons, steel crank, dowelled flywheel, etc. Carbs can be changed for 48s or 50s; the head needs to be full race, as does the camshaft, but the end result of all this effort is 185–200bhp. Throttle bodies and engine management should also be considered, as they really transform the Pinto. The real issue with the Pinto is the weight, although Burton Power has just introduced an all-alloy Pinto engine.

ESSEX V4/V6

FAST ROAD

The V4 is not the ideal engine for tuning and any efforts to increase its power are usually met with disappointing results. It's best to stick to a less restrictive exhaust and free-flow filter. The V6, on the other hand, is far more responsive. This is a great engine, but it's not without its faults. Firstly, the fibre teeth on the timing gear have a tendency to strip. Although the replacement steel timing gear is noisier, this really is a fit and forget solution and should always be done when undertaking a camshaft upgrade. Secondly, the heads have to be converted for unleaded, which is a good excuse for getting them uprated to stage 1 at the very least.

Carburation isn't an issue until serious levels of power are reached. It's a 38 DGAS Weber and can flow up to 180bhp, but you must replace the restrictive standard airbox with a free-flow filter. Group 1 racing Capris used the Weber DF15 and this gives excellent power.

With the filter, stage 1 heads, and free-flow exhaust the Essex V6 will have around 150–160bhp to play with.

FASTER ROAD/MILD COMPETITION

Stage 2 heads, a higher-lift camshaft, and an electric fuel pump will push power close to 180bhp. You'll also have reached the reciprocating limits of the standard componentry and 6,500rpm should be considered as the maximum.

SERIOUS COMPETITION

A pair of full-race heads, a race camshaft, and a serious exhaust system will raise the power to over 200bhp. Some full-race specification engines are delivering around 300bhp, and that's on a single 46 IDA Weber carburettor. Triple 40 DCNF Webers are also available, and on a full-race engine these can give anything from 240 to over 300bhp.

To ensure reliability, the crank needs to be cross-drilled and heavy-duty rod bolts should be fitted, as should roller rockers, screw-in studs, and forged pistons. Balancing this engine is tricky, but done properly it will help longevity. Even then, the rev limit should be 7,500rpm.

COLOGNE V6

FAST ROAD

The 2.0-, 2.3-, and 2.8-litre engines feature a short stroke, Siamese ported heads, and fibre timing gear. American-specification engines have always used three-port heads for emission control purposes. All are very smooth engines but they should not exceed 6,000rpm unless the rod bolts have been swapped for stronger ones and the rods have been stress-relieved and shot-peened. Doing this should allow the rev limit to be increased to 6,500rpm, and a rev limiter should be fitted. Stage 1 heads and a fast-road camshaft will add another 5–10bhp on the 2.8. If you opt for stage 3 heads and a hotter camshaft you can expect to see close on 200bhp. Free-flow filters and exhaust system will also liberate more power.

OTHER ENGINES

Although this is not quite moving into the realms of the unknown, you have to tread carefully. Swapping engines is a serious business and you'll need to ensure that the conversion is done correctly and

safely. Check with your insurance company first, and it's highly likely that an engineer's report will be mandatory. As with engine upgrades, engine swaps should only be undertaken in conjunction with the requisite suspension and braking upgrades. And always consult the experts or professionals before embarking on such a project.

There are numerous engines that can be fitted in the Capri's capacious engine bay. Here are some suggestions:

2.9EFI 12V

The most cost-effective way to improve power, and more importantly torque, is to fit the 2.9-litre Granada engine. It's an easy conversion for 2.8 Injection Capris as these cars already have the right fuel tank, engine mounts, and gearbox. Carburettors can be fitted (using the 2.3/2.8 inlet manifold) although the standard injection is the best bet. This can be set up on a rolling road.

24V COSWORTH V6

A very popular conversion and with good reason! Plenty of power, affordable, reliable, but it will require a good deal of engineering work. A bigger radiator will be required, as will a strong manual gearbox (not the Type 9) and clutch. The exhaust will also have to be specially fabricated and a number of other modifications are required.

COSWORTH YB TURBO

A relatively straightforward conversion and the power potential is simply enormous. Start at 200bhp and stop at around 550bhp!

ZETEC E

This is fast becoming one of the most-popular engine swaps. Although it's fitted to front-wheel-drive Fords, all the parts required to change it to rear-wheel drive format are available. Cheap, strong, and very tuneable, the Zetec E can deliver as much as 240bhp.

LOTUS TWIN-CAM 8V

The classic choice. This is a very straightforward swap and a good one too if you opt for the crossflow block and modular water pump kit. Swap the cams and 140bhp is yours, and there's the potential to push the power all the way to 190bhp. A massive range of replacement/tuning parts is available.

↑ **Triple downdraft Webers fitted to a Capri 280. (Gary Hawkins Photography)**

2.0-LITRE DOHC I4

Although usually judged to be something of a poor relation, this is a sensible swap for the Capri. The tunnel and propshaft will need to be modified, and you'll need an MT75 five-speed gearbox, but for your efforts you'll get a reliable twin-cam engine that runs a fully integrated management system and produces a healthy 130bhp.

FORD V8

Quite a few Capris have been fitted with a Ford V8 engine. New crated engines are available in various capacities and states of tune. However, getting the engine is the easy part! Modifying the shell, sorting the wiring, gearbox, drivetrain, etc, will take skill, imagination, and lots of cash. That said, the end result will be worth it.

ROVER V8

Lazy, lusty power! A very popular conversion, which turns the Capri into a proper muscle car with sounds to match. All the parts are available. The most common fitments are the 3.5 carburetted and 3.9 injected versions.

MAZDA ROTARY

Unusual, but very effective. Rotary specialist Silverstone Autosport has fitted a Mazda 13B normally aspirated engine into a Mk2 Escort rally car with astonishing results. The company can also fit this engine into the Capri. Currently, in full rally trim, the 13B is producing 300bhp. This is a very light engine (85kg) that sits low in the engine bay. Other modifications will be required.

FORD-COSWORTH BDA 16V

Do what Ford nearly did – fit the BDA. This engine is very expensive, very tuneable, and very well catered for. The basic unit has been produced in at least 15 different variations, including turbocharged. A normally aspirated 2.0-litre will churn out 240bhp and beyond.

DURATEC HE

The future's bright ... the future's Duratec! Popular for rear-wheel-drive kit cars, it can be supplied with all the parts to fit a rear-wheel-drive Ford such as the Capri, although some engineering will be required. With massive breathing potential and lots of uprated components available, 200bhp is easily on tap. When fitted with a better induction system and stronger internals that figure can rise to 300bhp.

Transmission

2000E 'BULLET'

The classic Ford four-speed gearbox. The 'Bullet' reference really only applies to the GT and RS specification gearboxes that had close ratios as standard. Alternative gear clusters are available (synchro and dog-engagement), as is a quickshift conversion and aluminium maincase and top cover.

TYPE E 'ROCKET'

Strong single-rail gearbox often referred to as the 'Rocket' box. Alternative gear clusters are available (synchro and dog-engagement, straight-cut gears), as is a quickshift conversion and aluminium tail housing and bellhousing.

TYPE F

As fitted to the 2.0-litre Capri. Has a cast-iron maincase, alloy tail housing, and side shift rods. No real performance potential.

TYPE 5

Four-speed gearbox fitted to V6 Capris (Essex and Cologne). In essence a larger version of the three-rail 2000E gearbox. No real performance potential.

TYPE 9

This is Ford's first five-speeder (complete with alloy tail housing) and is most commonly used for conversions to older four-speed Capris. Well worth considering. Alternative gear clusters are available (synchro and dog-engagement, semi-helical and straight-cut) as is a quickshift conversion and aluminium maincase, bellhousing, and top cover. The Type 9 is also available as a sequential gearbox (five- or six-speed). A low-ratio partial gearkit (which raises the first gear

ratio) can also be obtained on an exchange basis. The main part, if you're considering upgrading any part of the gear box, is the layshaft and needle bearing.

MT75

The gearbox that replaced the Type 9. Can be fitted with a quickshift conversion and alternative ration and straight-cut gears (five- and six-speed) can be obtained.

BORGWARNER T5

One of Ford's strongest production gearboxes and an ideal partner for a turbo YB conversion. Plenty of alternative gear clusters on offer, as is a quickshift and aluminium bellhousing.

Limited slip differential

Always a good idea on modified Capris. You're unlikely to find a Capri rear axle complete with LSD in a breaker's yard these days, so it's either look for a second-hand in the classifieds and budget for a rebuild, or buy new. Ask around and get the low-down on which type works best. The ratio will have to be chosen to suit the kind of use the car will get.

Clutches

When renewing a clutch check for oil contamination from a leaking gearbox seal or crank seal. Inspect the surface of the flywheel too. If this is scored it will need to be refaced. Check the condition of the thrust bearing (it's best to renew this) and look to see if it's operating correctly. A good-quality standard clutch kit will handle a modest power increase, although a better option is to fit a fast-road clutch. More highly modified cars will require a stronger clutch. The trade-off will be increased pedal pressure. For serious power outputs, you'll have to invest in a cerametallic 'paddle' clutch. If you've swapped gearboxes, it's likely that the thrust bearing and operating system will require modification. There's a plethora of clutch kits suitable for the Capri and its various engine options. Talk to the experts for advice.

↓ **3.9-litre Rover V8. (David Morgan Jones)**

↑ 503.6bhp Cosworth YB in a Brookland.
(David Morgan Jones)

→ Neat air intake for the turbocharger on this Cosworth YB-engined Capri.
(David Morgan Jones)

Interior

It's all a matter of personal taste and choice, of course, but Mk1 Capris and limited edition models are best served by keeping them as standard as possible. If modifications are undertaken, they should be done as sympathetically as possible. Hard-to-get items such as interior trim can very occasionally be found, but originality comes at a cost. If you can't track down original Ford material, contact the various specialist suppliers and work together to get as good a match as possible.

Less-well-equipped models can be easily upgraded with trim/equipment for a higher-specification version. If you're not overly concerned with originality, but at the same time you don't want to go too modern, a number of instrument manufacturers market gauges, switches etc that have period 'classic' styling. The same applies to seats. There are numerous period-looking aftermarket seats that will enhance the appearance of the interior and do a better job of holding you in. More often than not the rear seats can be retrimmed to match.

Unless you happen to own a Capri that's fitted with a sought-after steering wheel, a new leather- or suede-covered quality wheel is a great investment. Try to match the original wheel's diameter, as fitting a smaller wheel can result in too much kickback and greatly increased effort – especially if your car has manual steering. However, by choosing flat, semi-dished, or dished, it's possible to tailor the distance between your arms and the wheel perfectly.

There are numerous goodies available if you really want to personalise your Capri … gear knobs, handbrake gaiters, pedal covers, winder handles, door pulls, carpets, embossed floormats, sill finishers, seat belt covers, extra consoles, and so on.

It's possible to convert the windows to electric operation using a universal kit. Route any electrical cables through rubber grommets and ensure that the runs don't become trapped (the same applies to any other electrical equipment you might have added). Switches should be chosen so they match the original Ford switches, and they should be mounted where they're easily accessible yet look as if they were factory-installed.

As with all Fords of this era, the sound systems were far from being an audiophile's delight. There are numerous head units on sale and many will have MP3/ipod connectivity. Some will require an adaptor, most will slot straight in. Look for a unit that matches the car's interior styling and dash lighting.

If you want to keep the original look, it's possible to buy an MP3 adaptor that works via the cassette slot. Speakers are easily upgraded and with a little bit of thought they can be hidden behind existing speaker panels, or placed in the rear panel/parcel shelf and covered with special acoustic cloth. Similarly subwoofers and extra amps can be fitted out of direct sight. Of course, there are lots of specialist companies that will fill your Capri with sounds, screens, PlayStation/X-box, etc. The choice is yours!

Exterior

I admit I'm a bit of a purist when it comes to MkI Capris. When attempting to modify the exterior, try to think 'in period' and choose items that were around at the time. Cologne-type arches and body styling looks great. If you can find one, the louvred rear window cover looks good too. This was often partnered with rear quarter-window louvres.

The lighting can be improved, and it's a good idea to fit better bulbs or even a good-quality HID kit, but don't be tempted to make this too powerful as you'll incur the wrath of other motorists and the law, and it's likely that the original wiring and switching won't cope. A set of period-looking spots and fogs always look good. If changing wheels, opt for the retro look (Minilite, Compomotive etc). If you can get them, wide Lotus steels look great.

Later cars can mix and match components just as easily as the early cars. If you're into body styling, a wide range of GRP styling panels and parts are still being produced, including the X-Series, double XX, and MCR kits. RS/FAVO wheels always look right on the Capri and the right design of rear spoiler can often enhance the car's appearance. Done properly, colour-coding and window tinting (not too dark) looks good. Lexus-style lights are quite popular, as are angel eyes.

↓ **Lovely louvres.**
(David Morgan Jones)

← **Customised Capri.**
(David Morgan Jones)

CHAPTER 10
THE SUCCESSORS

As far as Capri enthusiasts are concerned there hasn't been a true descendant of the Capri. That's not to say that Ford didn't try – it did – but the models that attempted to follow in the Capri's tyre tracks drifted wide of the mark. They were all good cars in their own way; they just didn't manage to capture the spirit of the Capri, or, consequently, a decent share of the market.

Mercury (Fox) Capri

This wasn't a bad car. It was actually what the North American market needed at the time. What galled Capri enthusiasts was the fact that so soon after Ford had unceremoniously given the Capri the chop it went and used the Capri name on what was in reality a badge-engineered 1979 Mustang III, the car that was effectively the reason for the original Capri's demise. In production until 1986, the Mercury Capri – like the Mustang – was based on the Fox platform.

There were a number of different factory-produced variants marketed, including high-performance coupes and even some convertibles. Outside the factory a vast range of tuned and/or modified versions were produced.

When Mercury initially advertised the new Capri it made many references to the original (usually to highlight how improved the new car was). The Mercury Capri was only available as a hatchback, whereas the Mustang could also be obtained as a two-door coupe. A variety of engines were offered, including the 2.3-litre Lima four-cylinder (normally aspirated and turbocharged), 2.8-litre Cologne V6, 3.8-litre V6, and the 5.0-litre 'Windsor' V8. With the larger-capacity engines, performance wasn't an issue but handling was. If equipped with the RS suspension package it handled quite well, but not as well as the original Capri. The trim options were initially Base, RS, and

Ghia. In 1980 a 4.2-litre V8 Windsor replaced the 5.0-litre, and the 3.3-litre in-line six-cylinder replaced the 2.8-litre V6 Cologne.

Between 1980 and 1986 the Mercury Capri underwent numerous changes that were aimed at maintaining its appeal and sales; 1986 was the Fox platform's final year for the Mercury Capri (the Mustang continued using Ford's Fox platform for quite some time), which had matured into a rather good car. Like the original Mercury Capri, the Mercury (Fox) Capri was a good racecar and it did rather well in the Trans-Am series, winning the manufacturers' championship in 1984, 1985, and 1986.

Australian Capri

Having been used on the Mercury (Fox) Capri until 1986, in 1989 the Capri name was adopted by Ford of Australia for its Mazda Miata (MX5) rival. The Miata was not really an Australian Capri competitor as it was a two-door, rear-wheel-drive sports car, which had a purity of design and purpose. The Australian Ford Capri, which was available only as a convertible, and with its design penned by Ghia, was in fact based on the front-wheel-drive Australian Ford Laser/Mazda 323 mechanicals. It was sporting, but not sporty. Two versions were offered, the base model and the XR2. The base model utilised a SOHC 1.6-litre EFI Mazda engine, with the XR2 being powered by a DOHC 1.6-litre EFI Mazda that was also turbocharged. Only the base model could be had with a four-speed automatic transmission. In October 1990 the range was updated slightly and the power of the Base model was raised.

In April 1992 the range was revamped and the XR2 could now be had with or without a turbo. These were followed by the 'Clubsprint' turbo in July 1992 and the normally aspirated 'Barchetta'. The final updated model, the SE, was released in August 1993 as a Barchetta, an 'XR2' (both turbo and non-turbo

← Capri by name, but not by nature. The Australian Ford Capri. (Ford Motor Company)

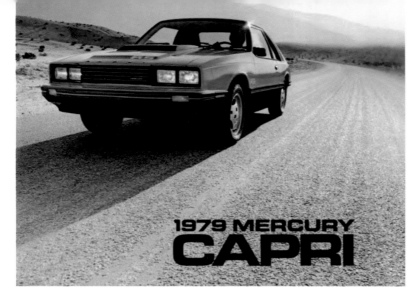

1979 MERCURY CAPRI

↑ **Although not an 'original', the Mercury Capri was a pretty good car. (Ford Motor Company)**

→ **Despite being a very good car, and a sales success, the Probe didn't capture the hearts of Capri enthusiasts. (Ford Motor Company)**

120 were exported to Singapore, Hong Kong, and Thailand. In 1994 only 232 Capris were exported to North America.

Ford Probe – first generation

As early as 1982 Ford began work on the next-generation Mustang, which was intended to be a sleek, fuel-efficient, front-wheel-drive car. The Mustang would share most of its components with the Mazda MX-6 and 626 models and would be a joint venture between Ford and Mazda. Mazda was a Ford partner, of course (Ford had a 25% stake in Mazda). Mazda purchased Ford's facility at Flat Rock in Michigan and it was here that the MX-6, 626, and the Mustang were to be built. However, when news of Ford's plans for the Mustang hit the public domain enthusiasts weren't exactly slow in showing their displeasure. Sales of the existing Mustang were on the increase thanks to a healthy dose of patriotism and a reduction in the price of crude oil. Thirsty V8 engines were back in fashion. Wilting under the weight of letters received from

versions), and finally as a 'Clubsprint' version (again, both turbo and non-turbo versions). Production of the Australian Ford Capri ceased completely for all versions in mid-1994. It was subsequently replaced by the imported US-built Ford Probe.

A total of 66,279 Capris were built by Ford Australia. Of these, 55,932 were left-hand-drive models built for the US market, with the remaining 10,347 being right-hand drive. From this group, 9,787 were sold on the Australian market, 440 were exported to New Zealand, and the remaining

Mustang traditionalists, who were bemoaning the fact that the company had even considered creating a Japanese-engined, front-wheel-drive Mustang with the lack of a V8 option, Ford capitulated.

It was now faced with something of a dilemma. Not only did it have to go back to the drawing board with the Mustang, but it also had to decide what to do with the redundant Ford/Mazda coupe that was ready and waiting to enter production. What Ford did was continue to run with this new model, but as an additional car in its range and not as a Mustang. To give it a new identity, Ford looked through its inventory of car names and picked one that was actually linked to the advanced concept car that the 'new' Mustang design had been inspired by. That name was Probe.

The first-generation Probe, a good-looking, aerodynamic, and stylish car, was sold in many markets and with a wide variety of trim options. In its home market, North America, where it was also manufactured, the Probe could be obtained in GL, LX, or GT trim. The GL was the base model and came with a 110bhp 2.2-litre SOHC, three-valve-per-cylinder Mazda engine and few extras. The LX had a good range of equipment as standard. Top of the range, though, was the GT, which featured LX trim, ABS, four-wheel disc brakes, and adjustable and uprated suspension, while its 2.2-litre engine produced 145bhp thanks to the addition of a Mitsubishi/IHI turbocharger and an intercooler.

In 1990 some minor restyling occurred and Ford's 140bhp V6 3.0-litre, 12-valve, 'Vulcan' EFI engine was added to the range. For 1991 the V6 produced a GT-rivalling 145bhp.

The Probe proved to be a major hit, proving that although it had been rejected by the hordes of Mustang enthusiasts, the concept, and its execution, was right.

Ford Probe – second generation

For various reasons, the first-generation Probe was more Mazda than Ford. With the second-generation Probe there was a much greater collaboration between the two parties, although it was still to share its mechanicals with the Mazda MX-6 and 626. Ford took control of the interior and exterior restyling, whilst Mazda worked on the engine and chassis.

Impressively, the teams managed to trim the Probe's weight by 125lb. This is even more impressive when one realises that the new version was 2in longer and several inches wider. The extra track and an extensive programme of track testing reaped dividends, as the Probe was an exceptionally fine-handling car. There were new engines too. The base model received a 2.0-litre, 16-valve, DHC Mazda engine that produced 115bhp. If you opted for the GT version you'd benefit from a new 24-valve V6, quad-camshaft engine, which delivered 164bhp. On sale in North America from August 1992, the Probe arrived on UK shores early in 1994.

Unfortunately for the Probe, as good as it was it soon came under attack from the new Mustang, which was released in 1994. The decline in Probe sales forced Ford to contemplate discontinuing production in 1996. In the end it managed to remain in production until 1997.

Ford Cougar

This was actually intended to be the third-generation Probe and was Ford's second attempt to reintroduce a sporting coupe in Europe. It was based on the Ford Mondeo and featured one of Ford's controversial 'New Edge' designs.

An American project that was developed in Europe but built in the USA at the Flat Rock plant, the Cougar was a very capable car, yet it didn't sell particularly well. Cars destined for the European market were transported to Ford's Cologne plant where a number of modifications were undertaken, such as re-branding it as a 'Ford Cougar' (for the North American market it was badged 'Mercury Cougar') and the fitting of European-specification lighting. Cologne also converted the UK cars to right-hand drive.

The UK launch took place at the 1998 British Grand Prix meeting. Three models were available, the 128bhp 2.0-litre 16V Zetec and the 168bhp 2.5-litre, 24-valve V6 and V6 auto. The options list was extensive. There was even an X-pack option on the 24V. A facelift model was introduced for the 2001 model year. When Ford restructured its plans and model line-up in 2002, the Cougar was dropped.

A fine car, but effectively a niche model, the Cougar never captured as many sales as it should have.

The 'other' Capris

LINCOLN COSMOPOLITAN CAPRI AND LINCOLN CAPRI

Ford's Lincoln division sold a model called the Capri from 1950 to 1960. Initially a special version of the Lincoln Cosmopolitan, it was a large coupe model. Between 1952 and 1955 the Capri became a model in its own right and was available in two-door, four-door, and convertible forms and was technically innovative. The Lincoln Capri was a major force in the original Mexican La Carrera Panamericana road race series in the 1950s and was very successful too. In its various Lincoln forms the Capri lasted until 1960.

FORD CONSUL CAPRI

Covered earlier in this book, the Consul Capri was a stylish coupe with a distinct transatlantic styling, good engineering, and a poor sales record.

MERCURY COMET CAPRI

In 1966 Mercury redesigned its Comet range and in doing so it replaced the Comet 404 with the Comet Capri. The Comet name was dropped in 1967 and the model became known as the Mercury

Capri. In 1968, and just in time for the arrival of the Mercury-badged Capri Mk1, the Mercury Capri was replaced by the Mercury Montego.

FORD SIERRA XR4I/XR4TI

Although not a Capri successor, the Sierra XR4i did impact on Capri sales, although not as much as Ford hoped it would. Whereas the Capri 2.8i was a sporty and nimble coupe, the XR4i was more of a GT car and its prime purpose in life was to transport four or five adults at high speed, safely, and over long distances. The XR4i was more refined and more sophisticated than the Capri … and cost £1,000 more than the Capri as a result. The Capri 2.8i was a great value for money, high-performance package, which comprehensively outsold the XR4i.

One definite successor was the XR4i's North American cousin, the three-door Sierra model, known as the Merkur XR4Ti, which was fitted with the 2.3L Lima turbo motor.

The parallels with the Capri are astonishing:

• Merkur brand dealers were Lincoln-Mercury dealers, just like with Capri.
• The Merkur XR4Ti was manufactured in Cologne.
• It suffered from similar confused marketing and brand identity issues.
• It used some specialist parts and there were

stocking issues, as with the Capri.

- Mechanics had to be specially trained to work on the Merkur XR4Ti, as they did with the Capri.
- Like the Capri, the Merkur XR4Ti suffered from an untimely and premature demise.
- And it was the Merkur XR4Ti which took over from the Capri in the British Saloon Car Championship and took saloon car ace Andy Rouse to one of his three championship titles.

The Capri of the future

The subject of a future Capri has been, and probably will continue to be, raised on a regular basis. Various ideas and designs have been mooted and displayed, some quite recently, and it does seem as if Ford will bite the bullet and relaunch this motoring icon.

Ford has already intimated that the next generation of the Capri is likely to be front-wheel drive and will be based on the Focus. A range of engines will be offered, although there have been suggestions that the launch engine will be a 1.6-litre TDCi.

Regrettably, however, Ford seems to be missing the point of the Capri – by a mile! The new Capri should not just be linked to the original by name alone, it should be linked by nature. There should be much of the original Capri's DNA coursing through the new Capri's veins.

Firstly, there is the thorny issue of styling. What made the Capri so special what that it looked so different and shared few familial links with other Ford cars. The Capri looked so new, so exciting, that it really did stand out from the crowd. What Ford should not be doing is designing a Focus coupe and calling it a Capri. The original Capri had personality … the designers need to remember this. And how many of the designers who will ultimately be responsible for designing the Capri have ever ridden in one, or even seen one in the flesh? Stylistically the new Capri needs to be a combination of retro and modern. Ford has already shown that it's capable of this with the Mustang – here is a car that ticks all the requisite 'modern' boxes, yet is an effective fusion of past and present. The new Mustang is a modern design triumph and a design classic. So when Ford's designers pen the new Capri they should take some of their styling cues from the original Capri and some from the current Mustang.

Secondly, there's the engineering issues and mechanical layout. Of course, the new Capri should be environmentally sound, it should be safe, and it should be cost-effective for the company too. Nonetheless, it should not be too perfect. Perfection is to be praised … but only in the right context. More often than not it's a car's quirkiness, its slightly flawed nature, which defines its very character and gives it its individuality. The classic car movement revolves around many cars that are far from perfect, yet they often exude character, charm, and personality. Obviously, the new Capri will be a modern design, but it shouldn't be too modern. Front-wheel-drive cars can be engineered in such a way as to provide an exceptionally rewarding, safe, and dynamic driving experience. Despite this, the new Capri should not go with the front-wheel-drive flow. It has to be rear-wheel drive. Only then will it have the correct balance, feel, and *joie de vivre*. If Ford wants to remind itself just how good the rear-wheel-drive experience can be, and how successful it is in a niche market, then it only has to look to one of its partner companies … Mazda.

Back in 1989 Mazda, a company in which Ford still has a small stake, was brave enough to reinvent the small sports car concept with the MX5. Over two decades later the MX5 is still hugely popular and a hoot to drive. Indeed, no top specialist motoring magazine's 'performance car of the year' (or similar) line-up is complete without the inclusion of the MX5. The MX5 is the perfect take on modern and retro. The concept has certainly been refined, yet the revisions have never taken the car too far away from its roots.

Thirdly, the new Capri has to be offered in a range of trim options and with a variety of engines to choose from. I remain unconvinced that the range should offer a diesel engine. That's not to suggest that diesels can't be sporty, they most certainly can. I'm just not sure that a Capri diesel is sending out the right messages. Try putting Mustang and diesel together and you'll begin to appreciate what I mean. If Ford continues to own the intellectual rights to Volvo's superb five-pot engines then that's good news. These are ideal for the new Capri and available in a variety of stages of tune, normally aspirated or turbocharged.

These are my personal observations, of course, but I remain steadfastly convinced that the new Capri has to be part of the present and yet rooted in the past.

APPENDIX
CLUBS, FORUMS, TRADE AND SPARES

The rise in popularity of the Capri has led to the emergence of numerous clubs, Internet forums, traders and specialist companies, all striving to help keep this iconic car where it belongs … on the road.

CLUBS AND FORUMS

The club and forum scene is particularly buoyant and caters for all aspects of Capri ownership including maintenance, social get-togethers, parts availability, technical advice, insurance, shows, concours, motor sport and so on. If you own a Capri, or are thinking of buying one, my advice would be to join one of the clubs, attend area meetings, visit the various shows, talk to owners, and make sure that you browse the forums. The Capri community is very sociable and extremely well informed.

TRADE AND SPARES

Thankfully, as it shares many components with other mainstream Fords the Capri's mechanical situation has always been good. Not that you're likely to find any Ford dealership carrying parts for any version of the Capri!

Fortunately, where Ford left off other enterprising traders and companies have taken over. Historically, the Capri has always been a car that enthusiasts tended to modify. In addition the Capri was raced successfully for decades, and it is still being raced in historic events. So not only can you obtain just about every mechanical component for the Capri, but you can also purchase uprated and/or modified components should you require them.

As far as body panels are concerned, the situation isn't quite as rosy. Nonetheless, the good news for Capri owners is that more and more panels are being remanufactured. If the panels simply aren't available, there are numerous companies that specialise in fabrication and restoration who can work wonders with metal. If you're unsure to whom you can entrust your pride and joy, then contact the clubs and forums for advice. Visit the companies too, as you'll be able to see the quality of their work first-hand.

Like genuine Ford panels, stocks of original trim have been steadily drying up, particularly for the early models. Thankfully this state of affairs is improving and demand has seen a number of trim panels become available, and the range is slowly expanding.

The list of clubs, forums and companies given opposite is not meant to be exhaustive, but it includes the better-known names etc, and should serve as a good starting point.

← **Wonderland International Classic & Sports Car Show 2010. (David Morgan Jones)**

Clubs

Capri Club International
www.capriclub.co.uk
capriclub@btclick.com
01386 860860

Capri Club Scotland
www.capriclubscotland.co.uk
capriscotland@aol.com
01555 894133

Scottish Capri Club
www.scottishcapri.co.uk

Capri Club Northern Ireland
www.capriclubni.co.uk
gourley_a@sky.com

Capri Club of Ireland
www.capriclubireland.com
capriclub_ireland@yahoo.com

Capri Club North America
www.capriclub.com
capri@capriclub.com

The Capri Car Club (Australia)
www.capricarclub.org.au
membshipsec@capricarclub.org.au

Ford Capri Car Club of New Zealand
www.fordcapri.co.nz

Capri Club of Queensland
www.capriclubqld.org.au
capriclubqld@yahoo.com.au

Capri Club Deutschland
www.capri-club-deutschland.de

Capri Club Passion (France)
www.ford-capri.net
contact@ford-capri.eu

Mansfield/Notts Capri Club
www.capriclub2000.co.uk
alan@capriclub2000.co.uk
01623 438967

Capri Mk1 Owners Club
www.caprimk1ownersclub.com
CapriMk1South@aol.com

Capri Mk1 Register and the
All Capri Club (Mid-Warwickshire)
www.fordcapriclub.com
information@fordcapriclub.com

Capri II Register
www.capri2register.co.uk
capri2reg@hotmail.com

The Ford Capri Laser Page
www.fordcaprilaser.co.uk

FordCapri.co.uk
www.fordcapri.co.uk
gilesfordcrush@yahoo.co.uk

Ford Capri Brooklands 280 and
280 Turbo
www.brooklands280.com

Tickford Owners Club
www.tickfordownersclub.com
tickfordownersclub@talk21.com

RS Owners Club
www.rsownersclub.co.uk
info@rsownersclub.co.uk
08702 406215

AVO Owners Club
www.avoclub.com
secretary@avoclub.com

Forums

Capri Power
www.capripower.co.uk

The Ford Capri Laser Page
www.fordcapriforum.com

RS2600 and RS3100
rscapris.proboards.com

Trade & spares

Aldridge Trimming
www.aldridge.co.uk
01902 427 474

Capri Care MK
www.capriclubmk.com
01908 365560

Capri Gear
www.caprigear.co.uk
01507 343 148

Caprisport
www.caprisport.com
01235 815207

East Kent Trim Supplies
www.classiccar-trim.com
01304 611681

Ex-Pressed Steel Panels Ltd
www.steelpanels.co.uk
enquiries@steelpanels.co.uk
01535 632 721

GMS Capri Spares
www.gmscaprispares.co.uk
info@gmscaprispares.co.uk
0191 377 1718

MWR Capri
www.mwrcapri.co.uk
mwrcapri@fsmail.net
01268 711658

Quoyloo Garage
www.quoyloogarage.co.uk
01856 841525
07766676379

Restore-A-Ford
www.restore-a-ford.co.uk
enquiries@restore-a-ford.co.uk
07717 861139

Retroford International
www.retrofordinternational.co.uk
01323 301022
07921102629

Revolution Capri Spares
stores.shop.ebay.co.uk/
revolution-capri-spares
revolution_capri_spares@hotmail.co.uk

Team Blitz
www.teamblitz.com
blitz@teamblitz.com

Tickover
www.tickover.co.uk
capris@tickover.co.uk
0208 298 1995

INDEX

References appearing in italics refer to photographs/illustrations etc.

2.8i Capri (Ford) 76-7, *77*, 79, 101, 128, *129*
12M Taunus (Ford) 44
'56 for 56' deal 9
230S Capri conversion 119
280 Capri (Ford) 78-9, 122, *129*
626 (Mazda) 152, *153*
911 (Porsche) 98

advertisements 26, 30, 36, 39, 40, 47, 64, 66
aerodynamics 71, 82, 106
AK Miller engines 64
Aldridge Trimming 126
Allard, Alan 115
Allard Motor Company (Turbosport) 115-16
American Sunroof Corporation (ASC) 50, 64
Ammerschlager, Thomas 104
Andrews, John 23
Anglia (Ford) 115, 121
Ariel Motor Company 82
Ashcroft, Peter 102-3
Aston Martin Motor Company 81, 82
Atom (Ariel) 82
audio systems 72, 77, 148-9
Australian Capris 52, *150*, 151-2
Autocar (magazine) 57, 58, 69
automatic transmission 48, 56, 58, 78, 120, 132
Automobile Manufacturers' Association 7
Autosport (magazine) 119
AVO (Advanced Vehicle Operations) 85, 86, 96, 108, 126

Bahnsen, Uwe 15, 59, 60
'Barchetta' Capris 151
'Batmobile' (BMW) 89, 105
BDA engines 27, 28, 29, 36, 85, 110, 146
Behra, José 97
Bell, Roger 82
Bergenkamp conversion kits 80
Bilstein suspension systems 76, 87, 90
BMW Motor Company 89, 104, 105, 107-8
Bobcat (Mercury) 62
bodywork restoration 132-7, *134-7*
bonnet 'bulge' see 'power-bulge'
Boreham facility 93, 94, 102, 103
BorgWarner transmissions 48, 120, 132, 147
braking systems 76-7, 87, 107, 132, 139-41, *140*
Braungart, Martin 93, 102, 103, 104, 105
Brembo braking systems *140*
British Racing and Sports Car Club (BRSSC) 100
British Saloon Car Championship (BSCC) 98, 98-101, 121, 155
Broad, Ralph 98
Broadspeed 98, *111*, *116*, 116-17
'Bullet' transmissions 146
Bullit conversions *116*, 117
Burton Power 144

'C'-shape rear window 17, *18*
Cabaret Capri (Ford) 75, 76, *129*
Calypso Capri (Ford) 75, *129*
Camaro (Chevrolet) 100
Cameo Capri (Ford) 75
Capri II (Ford) *54*, 55-69, 56-8, *65*, 127-8, *128*
Capri III (Ford) 70, 71-83, *72*, 74, *129*
'Capri Custom Plan' 27
'Caprice' convertible Capri (Ford) 123, *123*
Caprisport conversion 139, *140*
Car (magazine) 69, 82

Car and Driver (magazine) 47-8, *48*
Carbodies coachbuilders 123
'Cardinal' project 44
'Carla' project 71
catalytic converters 62
Chastain, Roger 64
Chastain S/3 option pack 64, *65*
Chausseuil, Guy 97
Clark, Roger 93, *94*, 96, 100
Clark, Stan *95*, 96
'Clubsprint' Capris (Ford) 151-2
clutch renewal 147
coachlining 60, 77, 78
Cologne engines 43-4, 49, 61, 67, 76, 87, *129*, *131*, 144
Cologne facility (Germany) 23, 38, 59, 61, 66, 93, 102-3
Colt (Ford)
    development of 12, 14-18, 19-21, 23-4
    images of *13*, *14*, *15*, *16*, *17*, *20*, *21*, *22*
'Comanche' tuning kits 121
'Comet' Capri (Mercury) 154
'Consul' Capri (Ford) 17, 18, 19, *19*, 123, 154
'Consul' Classic (Ford) *18*, 18-19
convertibles 123, *123*
cooling systems 107
Cortina (Ford) *13*, *15*, 18-19, *19*, 21, 79, 85, 120-1
Corvair Monza (Chevrolet) 10
Corvette (Chevrolet) 10
Cosworth engines 106, *106*, 110, 111, 145
Cougar (Ford) 153-4, *154*
Coupe (Audi) 77
Crayford *117*, 123, *123*
CSL Coupe (BMW) 105

dashboard design 41, *42*
decline of the Capri 125
'Décor' option packs 48, 63
Dekon Monza IMSA GT (Chevrolet) 112
DFV engine 13-14, 106
diesel designs 37, 155
Dohc engines 146
DRM series 79, 106, 108-111
'droop-snooted' design 71
ducktail spoilers 89, *91*, 106
Duckworth, Keith 13, 102
'dummy' side vents 41, 44
Dunton facility (UK) 18, 20, 23, 36-7
Dura-Spark ignition systems 65
Duratec engines 146

E.D. Abbott convertibles 123, *123*
East African Safari Rally 97
Eberspächer/Bosch turbo systems 80
electric window conversions 148
engine restoration/swapping 141-6
EPA (Environmental Protection Agency) 50, 62
Ertl, Harald 109
Escort (Ford) 78, 85, 93, 97, 108
Essex engines 27, 36, 39, 41, 61, 76, 131, *131*, 144
European Touring Car Championship 89, 104
Ex-Pressed Steel Panels 132
exhaust systems 118
Exterminator conversions *117*, 117

Fairlane Committee 9
Falcon (Ford) 10
Ferodo braking systems 87, 117
FF (Jensen) 93
FF4 Automobiles (New York) 97
FFD (Ferguson Formula Developments) 93, 96-7
FIA 85, 98, 105

Fiesta (Ford) 61
'Flowline' styling 16
Ford, Edsel (son of Henry Ford II) 50-1
Ford II, Henry 7, 9, 11, 12, *12*, 21-3, 50, 68
Ford Motor Company
    European unification of 20-3, 93
    in motorsport 12-13, 59, 75, 85, 92-113
Ford V8 engines 146
four-wheel-drive 93-7
'Frankenstein' S/3 Capri II (Ford) 64
Frey, Don 10
fuel-injection systems 50, 66, 76-7, 78
fuel tank design 34-5, 37
future of the Capri 155
FV9 camshafts 119

Garrett turbo system 81, 82, 122
Gauntlet, Victor 81
'GBX' styling 16
gearboxes
    automatic transmission 48, 56, 58, 78, 120, 132
    ratios 38, 41, 42, 61, 74, 87-8
    restoration/swapping 132, 146-7
Genk facility (Belgium) 23
'Ghia' models 55-6, *56*, 57, 58
Glemster, Dieter 97, 104
Goodyear tyres 37
Graham, Stuart *99*
Green, Basil 53, 112, 119-20
Group 5 racing (Zakspeed) 74, 75, 79, 81, 108-112, *108*, *109*, 113
GT4 Capri (Ford) 75, *129*
GT40 (Ford) 7
Gurney, Dan 10

Halewood facility (UK) 23, 38, 59, 61
hatchbacks 55, 62
Hayes, Walter 12-14, 23, 68, 89, 93, 102
Hella headlamps 88
Heyer, Hans 104, 105, 109, 110
Hill, Graham 104
Hitchman, John 18
Hockenheim (racing circuit) 109, 110
Holley Carburettors 63, 68, 119, 120
Hunt, James 100
Hurst, Dave 134-7

Iacocca, Lee 9-12
iconic status of the Capri 125
IMSA 111-12
'Injection Special' Capri (Ford) 78

Janspeed Motor Company 118
Jones, Mick 94
Jordar, Doctor Loyal 97

'K-Jetronic' injection system (Bosch) 76
Kent engines 27, *28*, 47, 48, 49, 56, *129*, 141-3
Kershaw, Geoffrey 122
Kevlar bodywork 110
Kranefuss, Michael 68, 93, 102, 104, 105, 112
Kugelfischer injection systems 88
Kwech, Horst 112

laminated windscreens 71, 127
Laser Capri (Ford) 76, *76*, *129*
Lauda, Nicki 109
launch of the Capri 24-5
'Le Cat' range 63, *63*
Le Mans 7
leaf-spring suspension 103, 106, 139, *140*
Lee, Barry 95
Lima engines 62, 65, 67, 151, 154

Lime Rock Park (racing circuit) 50
Lincoln Capri 154
Lincoln-Mercury franchise 47, 49, 64
Lindenburg, Peter 112
London-Sydney Marathon 97
Lotus engines 145
Luca injection systems 106
Ludwig, Klaus 69, 111
LuMo Motor Company 118-19
Lutz, Bob 81

Mako V8 Capri (Ford) 122-3
Mansfield, Rod 76, 86
marketing
    see also advertisements
    Europe 24-5, 27-8, 30-1
    US 46-8, 151
Mass, Jochen 104, 105
Matthews, Dave 98, 100
May, Michael 80
Mazda engines 146
Mazda Motor Company 151, 152-3
McPherson suspension systems 104, 139
Mercury (Fox) Capri 151, 152
Merkenich facility see Cologne facility
Michael of Kent, Prince 100
Miles, John 81, 105
Miller, Glenn 51
MIRA (Motor Industry Research Association) 89
Mitsubishi Motor Corporation 24
Mk I Capri (Ford) 41-9, 41, 42, 125-7
Modern Motor (magazine) 120
modifications 138-49
'Modular-Aerodynamic' design 71
Monte Carlo Rally 115
Monza (racing circuit) 98
Motor Magazine (magazine) 62-3
Motor Sport (magazine) 117
Motor Trend (magazine) 48-9
Motorcraft carburettors 64-5
Motorsport camshafts 120
Muir, Brian 105
Murdock, Norm 97
Mustang (Ford)
    comparisons with Capri 62-3, 66-8, 151
    development of 7, 9-11
    images of 8, 10, 11
    Mk II introduced 66-8
    in motorsport 111-12
    popularity of 9, 11-12, 14, 152-3
MX5 (Miata) (Mazda) 151, 155
MX6 (Mazda) 152, 153

Nader, Ralph 34
naming of the Capri 24
NASCAR 112
National Motor Vehicle Safety Act (1966) 34
Neerpasch, Jochen 85, 93, 102, 104, 105, 106
New Zealand Capris 52, 69, 79
Niehl facility (Germany) 85, 86-7
Nürburgring (racing circuit) 107, 109

Olthoff, Bob 112
option packs 31, 38, 42, 48, 63, 64
Oselli Engineering 119

paintwork options 41, 58, 60, 75, 77, 91, 120
Pantera (Ford) 47
parts 126-7, 127, 131
Pearson, John 77
Perana Capri (Ford) 53, 112, 114, 119, 119-20
Percy, Win 101
personalisation 27-8, 30-1
Pinto (Ford) 35, 47, 62, 67-8

Pinto engines 42, 46, 48, 49, 56, 61, 129-30,
    130, 143, 143-4
Piot, Jean Frances 96, 97
'Plastikbombes' 86
Popular Motoring (magazine) 77
'power-bulge' 36, 37, 41, 44, 88
power-steering 58
Prechter, Heinz 50-1, 64
pricing
    Europe 57-8, 78, 83
    US 47, 49, 62
Probe (Ford) 152, 152-3
production figures 83, 91
'Project Colt' 12, 14-18
'Project Diana' 55
'Project Redcap' 22
Prosyniuk, John 51
purchasing a Capri 125-9

quad headlights 41, 42, 71, 73

RAC (Royal Automobile Club) 100
Race Proved conversions 120-1
'Rally Cat' option pack 64, 64
rallycross 93-7
Rallye Sport (RS) Series 53, 84-91, 125
rallying 97-8
rear-seat accommodation 16-17, 30, 42
restoration of Capris 124-33
'Rialto' panels 60
Road and Track (magazine) 48, 49, 62
Road Test (magazine) 48
Robson, Graham 58
'Rocket' transmissions 146-7
roll-cage technology 109-110, 141
Rolt, Major Tony 93, 96
Roto-Master turbochargers 118
Rouse, Andy 101, 111, 155
Rover V8 engines 146, 147
R/S option packs 64
RS (Rallye Sport) Series 53, 84-91, 125
RS2600 Capri (Ford)
    development of 53, 85-9
    images of 50-1, 53, 84, 86, 88, 92, 126
    in motorsport 50-2, 103-4, 105, 113
    restoration of 125-6
RS2800T Capri (Ford) 79-81, 79, 80
RS3100 Capri (Ford)
    development of 89-91
    images of 89, 90, 91
    in motorsport 106-8, 111, 113
    restoration of 125-6, 134-7
rubbing strips 71

'S' model (Capri 'S') (Ford) 57-60, 59, 60, 127
Saab Motor Company 34
Saarlouis facility (Germany) 61
safety 33-5, 34, 35, 47, 49
sales
    Europe 38, 55, 56-7, 61, 78
    US 47, 48, 49, 65
Saunders, Simon 82
'Savage' Cortina (Ford) 120-1
SCCA (Sports Car Club of America) 97-8, 112
Scheel seats 87, 88
Schrick components 110
seat belts 34
'Series-X' option packs 69, 73, 74, 128
service intervals 71-2
Setright, L.J.K. 69
Sierra (Ford) 83, 101, 154
Silverstone (racing circuit) 98
Soler-Roig, Alex 104, 105
'Sonic Idle' carburettors 58

South African Capris 53, 112, 119-20
'Special' model ('Capri Special') 39, 39, 41
Spice, Gordon 99, 100
spoilers
    ducktail 89, 91, 91, 106
    front 71, 81
    rear 39, 64, 71
spot lamps 88, 91
Springalex steering wheels 87
steering wheel design 41, 72, 87, 148
Stewart, Jackie 25, 91, 104, 105
structural integrity 34
Stuck, Hans 105
Super Speed conversions 121, 121
suspension 24, 42, 76, 103, 104, 106-7, 132,
    139-40
SVE (Special Vehicle Engineering) 76, 82
SVO (Special Vehicle Operations) 68, 111-12
'Sweepstakes Special' (Ford) 51

Taunus (Ford) 21, 43, 44, 45, 46
Team Blitz 51, 52, 64, 97, 97-8, 112, 112
Theodoracopulos, Harry 112
'Thermactor' exhaust pumps 62
Thundersaloon series 102
Tickford 2.8T Capri (Ford) 81-3, 82, 83, 129
'Total Performance' programme 7, 9, 68
Tour de Corse 96, 97
Tour de France 97
Tour of Britain 100
Trans-Am Series 151
Transit (Ford) 22
turbo systems 80, 81, 116-17, 118, 122, 131
Turbo Technics conversions 122, 122
TÜV approval system (Germany) 74, 86
tyre pressures 139, 140
Tyrell, Ken 50

understeer 93, 96
unleaded petrol 62
Unsafe at any Speed (book) 34
Ur quattro (Audi) 93
Uren, Jeff 120-1

V6 Capri development 35-8
Vandervell bearings 119
Vantage (Aston Martin) 81
'VFM' (Value for Money) policy 57
Vinatier, Jean 97
Volvo Motor Company 34

Walkinshaw, Tom 100
Watts linkage system 139, 140
Weber carburettors 36, 68, 68, 69, 90, 118,
    130, 142-4, 145
Wells, Larry 97
Westlake engines 97, 102, 105, 106
Willment, John 120
Wolfrace Sonic alloys 76-7
wraparound bumpers 71, 72
WRC (World Rally Championship) 97

'X-packs' 69, 73, 74, 128
XLR models 31, 31, 32, 37, 38
XR4Ti (Merkur) 154-5

Young, Mike 121

Zakowski, Erich 108-9
Zakspeed Capri (Ford) 68-9, 74, 75, 79, 79,
    108-112, 108, 109, 113
Zephyr (Ford) 36, 120, 123
Zetec engines 145
Zodiac (Ford) 21, 36, 38, 123

ACKNOWLEDGEMENTS

There were many people who helped me put this book together. I apologise if I have omitted anyone!

Research: Jeremy Walton, Norm Murdock, Francis Ellingsworth, Vernon Witney, Dave Hill, Darren Revill, Ben Morley, Stephen Wickham, John Nevill, Glyn Jones, Kevin Hickling, Trevor Steadman, Richard Austin, Alan Allard, Geoff Kershaw, Steve Cash, Tim Richardson, Barry Priestman, Max Rokka, Len Bailey, Alan Daffin, Neil Bray, Dave Weir, Dave Hurst, Andrea Hurst, Kevin Blow, Mike Hargreaves, Jeremy Easson, Simon Ellis.

Photography: Gary Hawkins, John Colley, Chris Taylor/CTP, Chris Brown, Paul Kooyman, Jon Hill, David Morgan Jones, Norm Murdock, Dave Hurst, Flow Images, Ford Motor Company, Magic Car Pics, Capri Sport.

BIBLIOGRAPHY

Capri – Jeremy Walton - Foulis

Essential Ford Capri – Chris Rees – Bay View Books

Ford in Touring Car Racing – Graham Robson - Haynes

RS The Faster Fords – Jeremy Walton – Motor Racing Publications

Twice Lucky – Stuart Turner - Haynes

Ford Competition Cars – Frostick/Gill - Haynes

Cosworth The Search For Power – Graham Robson - Haynes

Ford Capri High Performance Models 1969–1987 – Chris Horton – W&G

Improve & Modify Capri – Lindsay Porter & Dave Pollard - Haynes

High Performance Capris Gold Portfolio 1969–1987 – Brooklands Books

Capri Muscle Portfolio 1974–1987 – Brooklands Books

The British Saloon Car Championship – Martyn Morgan Jones - Bookmarque